"This series is a tremendous resource for those wanting to study and teach the Bible with an understanding of how the gospel is woven throughout Scripture. Here are gospel-minded pastors and scholars doing gospel business fror   theo-logical feast preparing God's people to apply th   mind wholly committed to Christ's priorities."

BRYAN CHAPELL, Chancellor, Covenant'

"Mark Twain may have smiled when he wrote   you a short letter, so I wrote you a long letter.' But the truth of Twain's remark remains serious and universal, because well-reasoned, compact writing requires extra time and extra hard work. And this is what we have in the Crossway Bible study series *Knowing the Bible*. The skilled authors and notable editors provide the contours of each book of the Bible as well as the grand theological themes that bind them together as one Book. Here, in a 12-week format, are carefully wrought studies that will ignite the mind and the heart."

R. KENT HUGHES, Senior Pastor Emeritus, College Church, Wheaton, Illinois

"*Knowing the Bible* brings together a gifted team of Bible teachers to produce a high-quality series of study guides. The coordinated focus of these materials is unique: biblical content, provocative questions, systematic theology, practical application, and the gospel story of God's grace presented all the way through Scripture."

PHILIP G. RYKEN, President, Wheaton College

"These *Knowing the Bible* volumes provide a significant and very welcome variation on the general run of inductive Bible studies. This series provides substantial instruction, as well as teaching through the very questions that are asked. *Knowing the Bible* then goes even further by showing how any given text links with the gospel, the whole Bible, and the formation of theology. I heartily endorse this orientation of individual books to the whole Bible and the gospel, and I applaud the demonstration that sound theology was not something invented later by Christians, but is right there in the pages of Scripture."

GRAEME L. GOLDSWORTHY, former lecturer, Moore Theological College; author, *According to Plan, Gospel and Kingdom, The Gospel in Revelation,* and *Gospel and Wisdom*

"What a gift to earnest, Bible-loving, Bible-searching believers! The organization and structure of the Bible study format presented through the *Knowing the Bible* series is so well conceived. Students of the Word are led to understand the content of passages through per-ceptive, guided questions, and they are given rich insights and application all along the way in the brief but illuminating sections that conclude each study. What potential growth in depth and breadth of understanding these studies offer! One can only pray that vast numbers of believers will discover more of God and the beauty of his Word through these rich studies."

BRUCE A. WARE, Professor of Christian Theology, The Southern Baptist Theological Seminary

KNOWING THE BIBLE

J. I. Packer, Theological Editor
Dane C. Ortlund, Series Editor
Lane T. Dennis, Executive Editor

• • • • • •

Genesis	Mark
Ruth, Esther	John
Psalms	Acts
Proverbs	Romans
Isaiah	Philippians
Matthew	James

• • • • • •

J. I. PACKER is Board of Governors' Professor of Theology at Regent College (Vancouver, BC). Dr. Packer earned his DPhil at the University of Oxford. He is known and loved worldwide as the author of the best-selling book *Knowing God*, as well as many other titles on theology and the Christian life. He serves as the General Editor of the ESV Bible and as the Theological Editor for the *ESV Study Bible*.

DANE C. ORTLUND is Senior Vice President for Bible Publishing at Crossway. He is a graduate of Covenant Theological Seminary (MDiv, ThM) and Wheaton College (BA, PhD). Dr. Ortlund has authored several books and scholarly articles in the areas of Bible, theology, and Christian living.

LANE T. DENNIS is President of Crossway, a not-for-profit publishing ministry. Dr. Dennis earned his PhD from Northwestern University. He is Chair of the ESV Bible Translation Oversight Committee and Executive Editor of the *ESV Study Bible*.

PSALMS

A 12-WEEK STUDY

Douglas Sean O'Donnell

 CROSSWAY

WHEATON, ILLINOIS

Knowing the Bible: Psalms, A 12-Week Study

Copyright © 2014 by Crossway

Published by Crossway
   1300 Crescent Street
   Wheaton, Illinois 60187

Some content used in this study guide has been adapted from the *ESV Study Bible* (Crossway), copyright 2008 by Crossway, pages 935–1128. Used by permission. All rights reserved.

Cover design: Simplicated Studio

First printing 2014

Printed in the United States of America

Trade paperback ISBN: 978-1-4335-4098-1
PDF ISBN: 978-1-4335-4099-8
Mobipocket ISBN: 978-1-4335-4100-1
EPub ISBN: 978-1-4335-4101-8

Crossway is a publishing ministry of Good News Publishers.

VP			24	23	22	21	20	19	18	17	16
15	14	13	12	11	10	9	8	7	6	5	4	3	2

TABLE OF CONTENTS

SERIES PREFACE

KNOWING THE BIBLE, as the series title indicates, was created to help readers know and understand the meaning, the message, and the God of the Bible. Each volume in the series consists of 12 units that progressively take the reader through a clear, concise study of that book of the Bible. In this way, any given volume can fruitfully be used in a 12-week format either in group study, such as in a church-based context, or in individual study. Of course, these 12 studies could be completed in fewer or more than 12 weeks, as convenient, depending on the context in which they are used.

Each study unit gives an overview of the text at hand before digging into it with a series of questions for reflection or discussion. The unit then concludes by highlighting the gospel of grace in each passage ("Gospel Glimpses"), identifying whole-Bible themes that occur in the passage ("Whole-Bible Connections"), and pinpointing Christian doctrines that are affirmed in the passage ("Theological Soundings").

The final component to each unit is a section for reflecting on personal and practical implications from the passage at hand. The layout provides space for recording responses to the questions proposed, and we think readers need to do this to get the full benefit of the exercise. The series also includes definitions of key words. These definitions are indicated by a note number in the text and are found at the end of each chapter.

Lastly, to help understand the Bible in this deeper way, we urge readers to use the ESV Bible and the *ESV Study Bible*, which are available in various print and digital formats, including online editions at www.esvbible.org. The *Knowing the Bible* series is also available online. Additional 12-week studies covering each book of the Bible will be added as they become available.

May the Lord greatly bless your study as you seek to know him through knowing his Word.

J. I. Packer
Lane T. Dennis

WEEK 1: OVERVIEW

▲

To most Christians, the Psalms[1] are familiar (we read, quote, and sing them) but also foreign (we struggle with the original setting as well as certain geographic places, theological themes, ancient poetic forms, and possible musical terms—like "Selah"[2]). With 150 Psalms to cover, we certainly won't be able to cover each Psalm in depth. We will, however, cover main themes and significant connections to Christ.

The Psalms are often called "the heart of the Old Testament." This is not only because if you open your Bible to the middle (the "heart" of it), you will likely open to a psalm, but also because they work on our hearts. John Calvin said of the Psalms, "I have been wont to call this book not inappropriately, *an anatomy of all parts of the soul;* for there is not an emotion of which any one can be conscious that is not here represented as in a mirror." Psalms is a collection of 150 poems that express a wide variety of emotions, including: love and adoration toward God, sorrow over sin, dependence on God in desperate circumstances, the battle of fear and trust, walking with God even when the way seems dark, thankfulness for God's care, devotion to the word of God, and confidence in the eventual triumph of God's purposes in the world. From tearful laments to triumphant thanksgivings, these expressions of emotion serve as patterns to shape the emotions and actions of the godly of every age. (For further background, see the *ESV Study Bible*, pages 935–941, or visit www.esvbible.org.)

Placing It in the Larger Story

Throughout history, God has been fashioning a people for himself who will love and obey him, and who will express and nourish their corporate life in gathered worship. The Psalms (or Psalter) served as a vehicle for the prayers and praise of God's people in Israel, and Christians of all races today, who have been grafted into the olive tree of God's ancient people (Rom. 11:17, 24), can join their voices together with Israel in their worship. Put simply, the Psalter is our songbook for worship as well (see Eph. 5:19; Col. 3:16). There are indeed adjustments to be made, now that Jesus has died and risen—e.g., we do not offer bulls as "burnt offerings" (Ps. 51:19)—and yet Gentile believers in Jesus may rejoice with the people of God of all ages.

Key Verse

"Let everything that has breath praise the LORD! Praise the LORD!" (Ps. 150:6)

Date and Historical Background

The individual psalms come from diverse periods of Israel's history: from the time of Moses (15th or 13th century BC), to that of David and Solomon (10th century), down to exilic and postexilic times (e.g., Psalm 137).

One hundred and sixteen of the psalms have titles. According to those titles, David is the most common author: he appears in 73 titles, and the New Testament adds two more (Acts 4:25 for Psalm 2; and Heb. 4:7 for Psalm 95). Other authors include the Sons of Korah (11 psalms), Asaph (12 psalms), Solomon (possibly two psalms), and Moses (one). Other psalms do not identify the author at all. For a number of David's psalms we are given the context for the penning of a particular psalm (e.g., Psalm 3 was written after David fled from and then battled Absalom, see 2 Sam. 15–17). However, the historical context of most of the psalms is unknown or vague, which allows for an elastic application to every reader at all times everywhere.

Outline

The standard Hebrew text divides the Psalms into five "books," perhaps in imitation of the five books of the Pentateuch (first five books of the Bible). The psalm that ends each book finishes with a doxology, and Psalm 150 as a whole is the conclusion both of Book 5 and the entire Psalter.

Book 1 (Psalms 1–41)

Psalms 1–2 have no titles that attribute authorship (but see Acts 4:25 for Psalm 2); they provide an introduction to the Psalms as a whole. The remainder of Book 1 is made up almost entirely of psalms of David: only Psalm 10 (but see note on Psalm 9) and Psalm 33 lack a Davidic superscription. Prayers issuing from a situation of distress dominate, punctuated by statements of confidence in the God who alone can save (e.g., 9; 11; 16; 18), striking the note that concludes the book (40–41). Reflections on ethics and worship with integrity are found in Psalms 1, 14–15, 19, 24, and 26.

Book 2 (Psalms 42–72)

Book 2 introduces the first Korah collection (42–49, although 43 lacks a superscription), with a single Asaph psalm at Psalm 50. A further Davidic collection is found in Psalms 51–65 and 68–69, including the bulk of the "historical" superscriptions (51–52; 54; 56–57; 59–60; 63). Once again, lament and distress dominate the content of these prayers, which now also include a communal voice (e.g., Psalm 44; compare Psalms 67; 68). The lone psalm attributed to Solomon concludes Book 2 with the Psalms' pinnacle of royal theology (72; compare 45).

Book 3 (Psalms 73–89)

The tone darkens further in Book 3. The opening Psalm 73 starkly questions the justice of God before seeing light in God's presence; that light has almost escaped the psalmist in Psalm 88, the bleakest of all the psalms. Book 2 ended with the high point of royal aspirations; Book 3 concludes in Psalm 89 with these expectations badly threatened. Sharp rays of hope occasionally pierce the darkness (e.g., Psalms 75; 85; 87). The brief third book contains most of the psalms of Asaph (Psalms 73–83), as well as another set of Korah psalms (Psalms 84–85; 87–88).

Book 4 (Psalms 90–106)

Psalm 90 opens the fourth book of the Psalms. It may be seen as the first response to the problems raised by the third book (Psalms 73–89). Psalm 90, attributed to Moses, reminds the worshiper that God was active on Israel's behalf long before David. This theme is taken up in Psalms 103–106, which summarize God's dealings with his people before any kings reigned. In between there is a group of psalms (93–100), many characterized by the refrain "The LORD reigns." This truth refutes the doubts of Psalm 89.

Book 5 (Psalms 107–150)

The structure of Book 5 reflects the closing petition of Book 4 in 106:47. It declares that God does answer prayer (Psalm 107) and concludes with five Hallelujah psalms (146–150). In between there are several psalms affirming the validity of the promises to David (Psalms 110; 132; 144), two collections of Davidic psalms (108–110; 138–145); the longest psalm, celebrating the value of the law (Psalm 119); and 15 "psalms of ascent" for use by pilgrims traveling to Jerusalem (Psalms 120–134).

As You Get Started . . .

As mentioned above, the Psalms are divided into five "books." Read the final verses of each of the five books (Ps. 41:13; 72:18–20; 89:52; 106:48; 150:6). What do these verses tell you about the overall theme of the book of Psalms?

The Psalms cover a great variety of poetic forms or types—laments, hymns of praise, hymns of thanksgiving, hymns celebrating God's law, wisdom psalms, songs of confidence, historical psalms, and prophetic hymns. Read the brief definition of the psalm types.[3] Then read Psalms 1, 19, 103, and 135 and identify their type.

The church father Athanasius called the book of Psalms "an epitome of the whole Scriptures," and the Protestant Reformer Martin Luther called it "a little Bible, and the summary of the Old Testament." Spend a few minutes skimming the Psalms and making a list of Old Testament characters, stories, and themes found there.

Jesus taught us to read our Bibles with him in mind—"everything written about *me* in the Law of Moses and the Prophets and the Psalms" (Luke 24:44). "The Psalms" or "the Writings," that section of the Jewish canon which starts with the book of Psalms, bears witness to Jesus (John 5:39) and so can "make [us] *wise* for salvation" (2 Tim. 3:15). The Psalms are quoted by the New Testament authors more than any other Old Testament book. When Paul quotes from the Old Testament, one-fifth of his citations are from the Psalms. And in Paul's sermons in Acts, he often quotes from the Psalms. Look at his Acts 13:16–41 sermon. Note especially verses 33 and 35. Which two psalms does he quote? Then ask yourself, based on those psalms, what does Paul affirm about Jesus?

Take a few minutes to ask God to bless you with increased understanding and a transformed heart and life as you begin this study of the Psalms.

Definitions

[1] **The Psalms** – Our English title, "The Psalms" comes from the Greek word *psalmos*, which is a translation of the Hebrew word *mizmor* (a word related to a verb meaning "to play a stringed instrument"). The traditional Hebrew name for the book is *tehillim* ("praises"), which is related to the word "hallelujah" (that is, "praise Yahweh").

[2] **Selah** – There are several Hebrew words and phrases in the Psalms, such as "Selah" (e.g., 3:2, and 68 other times), "The Sheminith" (Psalm 6 title), "Shiggaion" (Psalm 7 title), whose exact meaning is uncertain. They are probably terms for musical or liturgical direction, and in some cases may be names of tunes or styles of chants.

[3] **Psalm types** – While we cannot know with complete accuracy the ancient categories for the psalms, the basic types of psalms can be summarized as laments (presenting a troubled situation to the Lord), hymns of praise (calling believers to admire God's attributes), and hymns of thanksgiving (thanking God for an answered prayer). There are also hymns celebrating God's law (speaking of the wonders of the written Word), wisdom psalms (exploring themes found in the books of Job, Proverbs, and Ecclesiastes), songs of confidence (enabling worshipers to deepen their trust in God through difficult circumstances), historical psalms (recounting and celebrating God's acts in history), and prophetic hymns (echoing themes found in the Prophets, especially calling God's people to covenant faithfulness).

WEEK 2: DOORWAY TO THE PSALMS

Psalms 1–18

▲

Psalms 1–2 are the "doorway to the Psalms" in that they open the Psalter by introducing two of its primary themes: submitting to God's word and God's king. As we enter into Israel's songbook, songs that were originally sung at the temple[1] are applied to every individual ("blessed is the man"; Ps. 1:1) for his own personal prayers and contemplations (on the Lord's law "he meditates day and night"; Ps. 1:2).

The Big Picture

The first 18 Psalms take us on a journey through a full range of emotions and topics related to them, concluding fittingly with personal praise for what God has done and will do: "I love you, O LORD, my strength. The LORD is my rock and my fortress and my deliverer, my God, my rock, in whom I take refuge, my shield, and the horn[2] of my salvation, my stronghold" (Ps. 18:1–2). (For further background, see the *ESV Study Bible*, pages 942–960, or visit www.esvbible.org.)

Read through the entire text for this study, Psalms 1–18. Then interact with the following questions and record your notes on them concerning this section of the Psalms.

Don't overlook the obvious. The Psalms are poems. Thus, they all employ beautiful imagery and voice great emotion. They also are structured in a certain way. In Hebrew poetry the most distinctive and pervasive organizing form of poetic art is parallelism. The three principal kinds are synonymous, antithetic, and synthetic. In a *synonymous* parallel the second half-line is identical or similar to the first. In an *antithetic* parallel the second half-line is opposite the first. In a *synthetic* parallel the second half-line imitates but also adds to the first. All three forms carry forward the thought of the first. Look at Psalms 3:1; 7:10; and 18:27. These are three examples of the three types of parallelisms—synonymous (echoes), antithetic (contrasts), and synthetic (completes). From the three verses above, which verse represents what type?

Read Genesis 12:1–3 and 2 Samuel 7:12–16. How do these two promises relate to Psalm 2? Then, read Acts 13:33, Romans 1:4, and Hebrews 1:5. What is said of Jesus in relation to these promises?

For the first (it won't be the last!) time in the Psalms, "foes" and "enemies" are mentioned in Psalm 3. Look at the superscription for Psalm 3. How does learning that David was the author, and that this psalm was tied to the occasion of Absalom's rebellion (2 Samuel 15–16), help you better understand the strong language and blunt and seemingly brutal requests? (For further help on this topic, see the *ESV Study Bible*, page 938.)

The superscription for Psalm 3 is the first in the Psalter. The superscription in Psalm 4 is the first psalm to add "to the choirmaster" as well as "with stringed instruments." Other psalms will say "to the choir" and list various other instruments besides the human voice, such as "for the flutes" (Psalm 5; compare Ps. 150:3–5). Tune names are also sometimes given, such as "According to the Sheminith" (Psalm 6) or "According to the Doe of the Dawn" (Psalm 22). What do such titles teach you about the nature and use of the Psalms?

As we shall see in our study of the Psalms, the Psalms are quoted more than 70 times in the New Testament. The apostle Paul quotes Psalm 4:4 in Ephesians 4:26. How does he apply it?

Psalm 5 is the first psalm to call God "King" (v. 2). This is the most pervasive metaphor for God in the Psalms: he is the God who rules the whole of creation. This psalm also provides the first instance of a psalm with prayers for the personal downfall of enemies. What does the psalmist ask God to do? Why?

Psalm 6:1 is a good example of a parallelism. What different words mean nearly the same thing? How does the second line move beyond the first?

The early church labeled Psalms 6, 32, 38, 51, 102, 130, and 143 the "Penitential Psalms." Psalm 6 is the first of these psalms. While we don't know the specific sin or sins he sorrows over, what does the psalmist ask God to do for him?

Poetry uses imagery; what are the images employed in Psalms 6:6–7 and 7:1–2? Why does God use so many metaphors, similes, etc., in the Psalms? More specifically, how does such imagery aid the forming and expressing of ideas?

Psalm 8 is a "hymn of praise." Notice that God is not praised for abstract attributes, but rather for what?

The Psalms teach us about God as well as about ourselves. What is said of "man" (human beings) in Psalm 8? How does the New Testament—namely

1 Corinthians 15:25–27; Ephesians 1:22; and Hebrews 2:6–9—apply this Psalm to Jesus? Compare also Psalm 8:2 with what Jesus said in Matthew 21:16.

In light of Romans 3 (phrases like "None is righteous, no, not one; . . . for all have sinned and fall short of the glory of God"; vv. 10, 23), when the psalmist asserts his innocence it may come across as self-righteous and presumptuous. Such claims are made in a few psalms in this section, including Psalms 4:1; 6:1; 7:3–5, 8; 17:1–5; and 18:20–24. Look at those psalms for a context in which to set those claims. What is the situation? How does that change the way you read phrases like "my righteousness" or "my feet have not slipped"? And, more generally, is it proper to make such claims of innocence? If so, when?

The Greek and Latin versions of Psalms 9–10 have these psalms combined as a single psalm, in part because, together, they follow a basically acrostic³ pattern. Moreover, there are thematic similarities. What do the two psalms have in common? How are they different?

Psalm 9 serves as an excellent summary of Psalms 1–18: that the Lord is a king who righteously saves those who trust in him by judging the nations who do not. From Psalms 9–18, a group called "the wicked" (also called "sinners," "scoffers," "wrongdoers," "ungodly," etc.) rises to the surface. For example, look at Psalm 10. Why does the psalmist ask God to arise and judge the wicked? What have the wicked done?

Psalm 10 begins with a question we all ask at times: "Why, O Lord, do you stand far away? Why do you hide yourself in times of trouble?" Look at Matthew 26:53; 27:43; Luke 23:14–16; and 1 Peter 2:23. How did Jesus wait for God's answer to this question? How does he serve as a model for you?

How is the question in Psalm 15:1 (asked twice, as a parallelism) answered in the rest of the psalm? Does anything make you uncomfortable about the answers? How does Hebrews 12 give a New Testament perspective on this?

There is a popular Christian slogan that "God loves the sinner but hates the sin." What do you make of that slogan in light of Psalm 11:5?

It would be fascinating to do a study on all the questions asked in the Psalms! A common question (asked more than 20 times in the Psalms), starts "How long?" In Psalm 13, "How long?" is repeated four times. What helps the psalmist wait? Can what helped him, also help you?

Psalm 18 is an adaption of David's song in 2 Samuel 22. In Romans 1:3 Paul writes of Jesus as "descended from David according to the flesh." Similarly, Mary sings of her Son as being given "the throne of his father David" and having an everlasting kingdom (Luke 1:31–33). Jesus fulfills the Davidic covenant (read 2 Samuel 7). Where in Psalm 18 is this covenant talked about? Also, where is another place in the New Testament (there are many!) where Jesus is called "the Son of David"?

Read through the following three sections on *Gospel Glimpses, Whole-Bible Connections,* and *Theological Soundings.* Then take time to consider the *Personal Implications* these sections may have for you.

Gospel Glimpses

SALVATION. When the Psalms (e.g., Ps. 3:1, 6, 7) speak of salvation from enemies, they prefigure our salvation through Christ from the ultimate evils of Satan, sin, and death (Heb. 2:14–15). By means of the resurrection (Acts 3:13–15), God the Father delivered Jesus from his enemies, and that is the basis of our deliverance (Rom. 4:25). As sinners ("there is none who does good"; Ps. 14:1), we cannot stand before a holy God—"evil may not dwell with you" (Ps. 5:4). Christ's perfect holiness alone allows us to come into God's presence (Heb. 10:19–22).

BLESSING THE RIGHTEOUS. God's commitment to bless the righteous, as seen throughout the Psalms (e.g., Ps. 1:1), is supremely shown when he blesses Jesus, the perfectly righteous man, by raising him from the dead (Phil. 2:10–11). The blessings of Psalms are therefore for all Christians as well.

YOUR RIGHTEOUSNESS. Paul rightly uses Psalm 5:9 in Romans 3:13 as part of his argument that both Jews and Gentiles are under the power of sin. The two previous verses from Psalm 5 speak of how the genuinely godly recognize that they come before God only through "the abundance of your steadfast love" (v. 7) and "your righteousness" (v. 8), and thus they pray that God will "lead" them to walk in the "way" that is morally "straight" (v. 8). The righteous recognize that the only way to walk in righteousness is through the power of God.

19

Whole-Bible Connections

ANOINTED. Samuel anointed both Saul (1 Sam. 10:1) and David (16:13), setting them apart to be king. The king's task was to rule Israel and to embody covenant faithfulness. God used David and other Israelite kings to protect his people against enemies. The word "Messiah" comes from transliterating the Hebrew word for "Anointed," and the word "Christ" comes from translating "Anointed" into Greek. Israel's anointed kings prefigure Jesus Christ, who is enthroned after his resurrection (Acts 13:33), now rules over all the nations (Matt. 28:18; Eph. 1:21) on behalf of his people (Eph. 1:20–22), and will one day judge those who reject his rule. Salvation or judgment depends on one's relation to this anointed Son (Ps. 2:7, 12; 18:50; John 3:36).

DOMINION. Psalm 8:6 sings of man's "dominion over the works" of God's creation. In Genesis 1:28–30, God gave Adam dominion over the garden of Eden. Yet, due to his disobedience, Adam's and his posterity's dominion was diminished (Rom. 5:12–21). Through Jesus' resurrection and ascension (Heb. 2:5–9), he entered into dominion over the world (see 1 Cor. 15:42–49; Eph. 1:22).

HOPE OF EVERLASTING JOY. As in Psalms 49:15 and 73:24–26, Psalm 16:9–11 is a clear affirmation that the human yearning to be near to God and to know the pleasure of his welcome forever, beyond the death of the body, finds its answer in the covenant. Peter cites Psalm 16:8–11 in his Pentecost sermon (Acts 2:25–28), applying the verses to the resurrection of Jesus; Paul uses Psalm 16:10 in his thematically similar sermon (Acts 13:35). If the apostles meant that David's words were only a prediction of the death and resurrection of Jesus, it is difficult to know what function the psalm could have played in ancient Israel: the congregation would have scratched their heads in puzzlement every time they sang it. However, the puzzlement goes away if the psalm is seen as cultivating the hope of everlasting glory, with the resurrection of Jesus (the "holy one" par excellence) as the first step in bringing this hope to fruition (see Rom. 8:23).

THE NATIONS' PRAISE. After Psalms 3–17, Psalm 18 describes God's rescue for the righteous. The imagery here is awesome (e.g., "He bowed the heavens and came down; thick darkness was under his feet. He rode on a cherub and flew; he came swiftly on the wings of the wind"; vv. 9–10). The action culminates in God's anointed king praising God among the nations (vv. 49–50). The "nations" (i.e., Gentiles) are mentioned throughout Psalms 1–18, often as those who have rejected and revolted against God and his ways—"Why do the nations rage?" (Ps. 2:1; compare Psalm 9). However, Paul employs Psalm 18:49 in Romans 15:9 as a part of his proof that it was always God's plan that the Gentiles should receive the light, especially through the Davidic line (Ps. 18:50; compare 2 Sam. 7:12–16), of which Jesus is the ultimate heir. The nations now belong to Jesus (Ps. 2:8; compare Gen. 12:1–3), and so they sing his praises (Ps. 18:43, 49).

Theological Soundings

RIGHTEOUS. This term can be defined in various ways depending on the context. In some contexts, "righteousness" is seen as one of God's distinctive attributes, the quality of being morally right and without sin. In that connection, the Son of God displayed righteousness throughout his earthly life, and we are only righteous when God imputes the righteousness of Jesus Christ to those who trust in him. However, the term "righteous" in the Psalms usually refers more generally to those who are innocent of a specific sin or in contrast to certain sinners (their oppressors). Moreover, the righteous are the humble who voice their troubles to God in total dependence on his assistance.

RIGHTEOUS JUDGE. God is "a righteous judge" (Ps. 7:11), to whom all the peoples of mankind, and not only Israel, are accountable (vv. 7, 8); thus his "anger" (v. 6) and "indignation" (v. 11) are directed against those who threaten his faithful ones (the "righteous," v. 9; and the "upright in heart," v. 10). In English usage the word "judge" tends to focus more on condemning than on rescuing; in the Psalms, however, judging is usually a saving action—God intervening on behalf of the innocent and oppressed. The particular salvation or deliverance, then, is part of God's larger project of putting the whole world back in right order (v. 9).

THE LORD. The covenant name for God—LORD (Yahweh)—was given specifically to Israel, but it is "majestic . . . in all the earth" (Ps. 8:1). This name is mentioned 698 times in the Psalms. The psalms are LORD-centered, monotheistic songs! That is, they praise the one true Creator,[4] the maker of heaven and earth and ruler of all things. In the Psalms, Yahweh alone (no other gods) speaks, acts, sees, hears, and answers.

Personal Implications

Take time to reflect on the implications of Psalms 1–18 for your own life today. Consider what you have learned that might lead you to praise God, repent of sin, and trust in his gracious promises. Make notes below on the personal implications for your walk with the Lord of the (1) *Gospel Glimpses*, (2) *Whole-Bible Connections*, (3) *Theological Soundings*, and (4) this passage as a whole.

1. Gospel Glimpses

2. Whole-Bible Connections

3. Theological Soundings

4. Psalms 1–18

> ### As You Finish This Unit . . .

Take a moment now to ask for the Lord's blessing and help as you continue in this study of the Psalms. Take a moment also to look back through this unit of study, to reflect on a few key things that the Lord may be teaching you—and perhaps to highlight and underline these things to review again in the future.

Definitions

[1] **Temple** – There are many names for the temple used in the Psalms (house, tent, sanctuary, etc.). In the Old Testament, the temple is the place where God "sits enthroned" (Ps. 9:11; 22:3; 1 Sam. 4:4) as king forever especially over his people.

[2] **Horn** – The horn, as in "the horn of my salvation" (Ps. 18:2) or "lift up your horn" (Ps. 75:4), is a symbol of power and strength derived from the image of the horns of an animal, such as the wild ox (see 1 Kings 22:11; Zech. 1:18–21). God's "horn" symbolizes his anointed king through whom he asserts his power.

[3] **Acrostic** – A regular sequence of letters from an alphabet used to form a literary composition. Thus, for a psalm with an acrostic pattern, each line or stanza (as in Psalms 9–10) might begin with successive letters of the Hebrew alphabet.

[4] **Creator** – The Lord, the covenant God of Israel, is the creator and owner of all. He is the one who "founded" the world (Ps. 24:2; compare Gen. 1:1–2:3).

Week 3: Love the Lord, All You His Saints

Psalms 19–31

The Place of the Passage

The book of Psalms is a "collection of collections" of poetic prayers. Psalms 19–31 demonstrate the great diversity of forms and themes found in the Psalter, such as private and public petitions and praises, laments, and doxologies.

The Big Picture

As Psalm 18 began with an exclamation of "love" ("I love you, O LORD, my strength"; v. 1), so Psalm 31 ends, "Love the LORD, all you his saints!"; v. 23). The Lord is to be loved because the Lord alone can save (e.g., Psalms 9; 11; 16; 18). (For further background, see the *ESV Study Bible*, pages 960–975 or visit www.esvbible.org.)

> ## Reflection and Discussion

Read through the entire text for this study, Psalms 19–31. Then interact with the following questions concerning this section of the Psalms and record your notes on them.

Look at what is said about the written Word of God in Psalm 19:7–11. What synonyms are used for it? Find the verb "is" (also "are"). What "is" the Word?

Psalms 20–21 are "royal psalms" because they are concerned with the Davidic monarchy as the vehicle of blessing for the people of God. Psalm 20 is a prayer and Psalm 21 is a thanksgiving; both relate to the Messiah, the ultimate heir of David. How so? What pattern in these psalms was fulfilled in the life of Jesus?

In our previous lesson we encountered a "hymn of praise" (Psalm 8). Psalm 22 is the emotional opposite. It is a lament—a poem where a psalmist lays his troubled situation before the Lord, asking him for help. (As much as a third of the Psalter consists of laments.) In Psalm 22, how does David ask God to help? Why? In the passion narrative, Matthew's Gospel presents Jesus as a thoroughly innocent and faithful man who is brutally and unjustly executed.

Read Matthew 27:35–46 and fill in the chart below, showing where Matthew's account refers back to the verses listed here from Psalm 22:

Psalm 22	Matthew 27
Psalm 22:18	
Psalm 22:7	
Psalm 22:8	
Psalm 22:1	

Psalm 23 is a "psalm of confidence." David praises God for his presence, provision, and protection. What images does he use for each of those divine actions?

Based on the creation pattern of Genesis 1, certain psalms were assigned to each day of the week for temple worship. For example, Psalm 93 was sung on the sixth day and Psalm 92 on the seventh. With Genesis 1 as your guide, what day do you think Psalm 24 was assigned to, and why?

Psalm 25 is a lament, structured in an acrostic pattern. However, it doesn't end in the confident way most laments do, and it includes penitential elements. What does David ask God to do for him?

In Psalms 25–26, we again hear the language of personal integrity and innocence (e.g., Ps. 25:21 and nearly every verse of Psalm 26). How do such claims
fit with petitions for forgiveness ("For your name's sake, O LORD, pardon my
guilt, for it is great"; Ps. 25:11), pleas for redemption ("Redeem[1] me, and be gracious to me"; Ps. 26:11b), and temple worship ("altar" and "house"; Ps. 26:6–8)?

Although some of the psalms are didactic (instructional), overall the Psalter
is not a catechism but a doxological confession of faith. As such, we *see* what
genuine faith looks like. In Psalm 27, what is the picture of faith? In Psalm 29,
what is the picture of praise?

In the Psalms, theology is taught indirectly and implicitly and often through
imagery. In some psalms God is depicted as a king, warrior, judge, father, and
even a protective mother bird. What image is used for God in Psalm 28? What
does that teach you?

A "hymn of thanksgiving" is a psalm that thanks God for his answer to a petition. Some of these psalms are communal (e.g., Psalm 9) while others are individual, such as Psalm 30. What does Psalm 30 thank God for?

Psalm 31 is a lament that seeks help from God for a faithful person worn out with trouble and beset by "enemies" who want to do him harm (vv. 4, 8, 11, 13, 15, 18, 20). Sometimes it is difficult to connect such psalms directly to our lives. However, the psalmist's trust transcends time. How does he exhibit personal faith in God? How did Jesus do the same (Luke 23:46)?

Read through the following three sections on *Gospel Glimpses*, *Whole-Bible Connections*, and *Theological Soundings*. Then take time to consider the *Personal Implications* these sections may have for you.

Gospel Glimpses

LAW. The "law of the LORD" referenced in Psalm 1:2 and Psalm 19:7 speaks of the Torah—God's covenant instruction through Moses. Although some may use the law as a means of self-promotion, that is not what Psalm 19:12–14 teaches. Instead, meditation on the law should lead us to reflect on our own sins, known and unknown; to rely on God's forgiveness (justification[2]); and to seek God's protection from sin's dominion (sanctification[3]).

GOOD SHEPHERD. Psalm 23 begins "the LORD is my shepherd." In the Gospel of John, Jesus calls himself "the good shepherd" (John 10:11–18, 27–29). As the good shepherd, Jesus embodies God's care for his people, including the ultimate act of care—laying down his life for his sheep. Like the psalmist of Psalm 22, Jesus suffered physical, emotional, and spiritual pains. These sacrificial sufferings on our behalf brought salvation for us and adoration to him (Heb. 2:10–12).

Whole-Bible Connections

SINGING WITH JESUS. By expressing the emotional heights and depths in human response to God, the Psalms provide a permanent treasure for God's people to use for expressing their needs and praises, both corporately and individually. As the representative man, Christ experienced our human condition, yet without sin, and so the Psalms become his prayers to God, as seen in Hebrews 2:12. Psalm 22, from which that verse quotes, is associated with Jesus' death (e.g., Ps. 22:1, 16–18) and resurrection (vv. 19–24). The resurrected Messiah, his suffering completed, calls his "brothers" (those united to him by faith) to join him in worship. The Psalms are thus to be seen as Christ's words, and through our union with him they become ours.

SACRIFICES. The Psalms employ the language of the Old Testament sacrificial system—"offerings," "burnt sacrifices," "be acceptable," etc. Under the old covenant, sacrifices were the means by which the worshiper received assurance of God's love and devoted himself to God. Under the new covenant, Christians can "walk in love" (Eph. 5:2) and moral purity ("as children of the light"; v. 8) because "Christ loved us and gave himself up for us, a fragrant offering and sacrifice to God" (5:2).

Theological Soundings

REVELATION. Psalm 19 focuses on God's general (creation) and specific (the written Word) revelation. Together with Psalms 1 and 119 these psalms put forth the view (shared in the New Testament; 2 Tim. 3:14–17; 2 Pet. 1:16–21) that the Bible is perfect, authoritative, and sufficient. In Romans 1:18–25 and 10:18–19, Paul teaches that everyone has received some revelation from God and everyone is thus accountable before God.

THE WICKED. The Old Testament recognizes that the pious commit sins, even grievous ones, and it makes provision for them without calling such people "wicked" (see Ps. 32:6). It tends to reserve terms like "unfaithfulness" or "wicked" for the actual turning of the heart's fundamental loyalty away from God, as in idolatry (Ps. 44:20) or in persecution of the godly. The wicked are not simply people who commit sins (even the faithful do that; see Ps. 32:6), but are those who oppose God and his people with deceit and treachery. The Psalms generally recognize that God will indeed hold the wicked accountable for their deeds. The pious wish to see God's justice vindicated, when those who defy his rule receive their due, and they do not want to suffer when the judgment falls (see 2 Thess. 1:9–10).

Personal Implications

Take time to reflect on the implications of Psalms 19–31 for your own life today. Consider what you have learned that might lead you to praise God, repent of sin, and trust in his gracious promises. Make notes below on the personal implications for your walk with the Lord of the (1) *Gospel Glimpses*, (2) *Whole-Bible Connections*, (3) *Theological Soundings*, and (4) this passage as a whole.

1. Gospel Glimpses

2. Whole-Bible Connections

3. Theological Soundings

4. Psalms 19–31

Take a moment now to ask for the Lord's blessing and help as you continue in this study of the Psalms. Take a moment also to look back through this unit of study, to reflect on a few key things that the Lord may be teaching you—and perhaps to highlight and underline these things to review again in the future.

Definitions

[1] **Redeem** – Generally conveys the idea of rescue and protection, especially when the object is God's people (e.g., Ps. 44:26; 111:9; 130:7–8) or a faithful worshiper (e.g., Ps. 34:22; 55:18; 71:23). In some places it carries the idea of exchanging a substitute or ransom—the act of buying back someone who had become enslaved or something that had been lost to someone else (e.g., Ex. 13:13; Lev. 27:27–28). Through his death and resurrection, Jesus purchased redemption for all believers (Col. 1:13–14).

[2] **Justification** – The act of God's grace in bringing sinners into a new covenant relationship with himself and counting them as righteous before him through the forgiveness of sins (Rom. 3:20–26).

[3] **Sanctification** – The process of being conformed to the image of Jesus Christ through the work of the Holy Spirit. This process begins immediately upon regeneration and continues throughout a Christian's life.

WEEK 4: SURROUNDED BY STEADFAST LOVE

Psalms 32–41

▲

The Place of the Passage

Psalms 1–3 introduce us to a God who teaches, elects, and saves. The remainder of the psalms in Book 1 (Psalms 4–41) focus on David's deliverance from troubles, culminating in God's deliverance from sin (Psalm 32) and enemies (Psalm 41).

The Big Picture

In Psalms 32–41, the psalmists exalt in God's salvation—his rescue of the righteous from sin and the wicked. (For further background, see the *ESV Study Bible*, pages 976–989, or visit www.esvbible.org.)

Reflection and Discussion

Read through the entire text for this study, Psalms 32–41. Then interact with the following questions concerning this section of the Psalms and record your notes on them.

Psalms like Psalm 32 sing of forgiveness. Martin Luther called such Psalms "the Pauline psalms" because they reminded him of Paul's theology of the forgiveness of sins (e.g., Paul uses Psalm 32:1–2a in Rom. 4:6–8 to show that "not counting sin" [which he treats as another way of counting righteousness] has always been done "apart from works"). How is the forgiveness of sins illustrated? Look at verse 11. What does the forgiveness lead to?

Psalm 34 is another psalm that follows an acrostic pattern. Due to verse 8, "Oh, taste and see that the LORD is good!" Origen (AD 185–254) claimed that Psalm 34 was sung as a communion hymn in the early church. However, how does Peter use verses 8–9, 12–16 in 1 Peter 2:3; 3:12?

Psalm 35 shows how the faithful should pray when they know that malicious people are seeking to harm them. The prayer recounts the evil schemes of the persecutors and asks God to fight on behalf of his faithful one—"Draw the spear and javelin against my pursuers!" (v. 3a). Since this is God's inspired Word, let's assume such petitions are proper for God's people to pray. Praying for such divine judgments is one thing; rejoicing in them (vv. 9–10, 27–28) is another thing altogether. What are some reasons for such rejoicing (see especially vv. 7–8, 11–16; compare John 15:25 on Jesus' use of Ps. 35:19)?

The LORD's "steadfast love" is a major theme in the Psalms. According to Psalm 36:7–9, how is that attribute illustrated?

Psalm 37 is another acrostic. It is also a "wisdom psalm" because it shares themes found in the wisdom literature of the Bible—in the books of Job, Proverbs, Ecclesiastes, and the Song of Songs. The opening stanza establishes the overall theme of the righteous persevering through persecutions (vv. 1–4). First, what shall happen to the wicked? Second, what shall happen to the righteous? Third, in the meantime, what should the righteous do?

When the psalmist writes, "those who wait for the LORD shall inherit the land" (Ps. 37:9), "the meek shall inherit the land" (v. 11), and "The righteous shall inherit the land" (v. 29), what piece of real estate is he talking about? Jesus uses the first half of verse 11 in the third beatitude (Matt. 5:5). Is he referring to the same land?

The title of Psalm 38 associates the psalm with "the memorial offering." This is the portion of the grain offering that the priest burns on the altar (Lev. 2:2). Its purpose was to "remind" God that the worshiper had consecrated these gifts of God's own abundant providence and to remind the worshiper of his sins. What are the synonyms for sin in Psalm 38:1–8? What are the images for iniquities? In your own words and in your own life, how would you describe sin? Take a poetic stab at it!

Knowledge of self is rooted in our knowledge of God. In Psalm 39, what should we know about ourselves in light of God?

Admission and confession of sin are major themes in Psalms 38–41. List some verses to this effect. Also list verses that state the remedy to our sin situation.

Read through the following three sections on *Gospel Glimpses*, *Whole-Bible Connections*, and *Theological Soundings*. Then take time to consider the *Personal Implications* these sections may have for you.

Gospel Glimpses

STEADFAST LOVE. The Hebrew word *hesed* ("steadfast love") refers to God's covenant love with and for his people. This term is used 123 times in the Psalms! Confidence in the steadfast love of God, as revealed in the covenant[1] (Ex. 34:6), leads to a trusting expectation of salvation and God's bountiful blessing: "But I have trusted in your steadfast love; my heart[2] shall rejoice in your salvation. I will sing to the LORD, because he has dealt bountifully with me" (Ps. 13:5–6; see 32:10). Similarly, those who receive God's salvation through faith in Christ (Rom. 5:2; Eph. 2:8–9) will also receive all the heavenly blessings of that saving relationship (Eph. 1:3).

DELIVERANCE. The Psalms speak openly about the realities fallen humans face—enemies (e.g., Ps. 37:9), death (e.g., Ps. 39:4), and God's wrath (e.g., Ps. 38:1). Only Jesus, through his resurrection and return, can deliver God's people from enemies (Col. 2:15; Rev. 20:11–21:8), death (1 Cor. 15:12–26, 35–58), and divine judgment (John 3:36; Rom. 5:1).

Whole-Bible Connections

SIN OFFERING. Psalm 40:6b reads, "Burnt offering and sin offering you have not required." While that seems like a stunning statement, it was not uncommon in the Old Testament for categorical correctives to be given to any who might think that the sacrificial system worked automatically, apart from expressing faith, repentance, and obedience (see Ps. 50:8–15; 51:16–19; Prov. 14:9; Isa. 1:11–17). This is probably why Hebrews 10:5–7 uses Psalm 40:6–8, because its audience was tempted to abandon their specifically Jewish Christianity and revert to "ordinary" Judaism, with its sacrifices, thinking they would still be pleasing God. They must see the sacrifices as a means of furthering God's larger purposes, not as producing effects on their own.

SAINTS. The term "saints" is used in both the Old and New Testaments to refer to God's people (Ps. 85:8; Eph. 1:1)—those he has "set apart" for himself from the nations to "be holy" as God is holy (Lev. 20:7–8; 1 Pet. 1:15–16). The term is used a dozen times in the Psalms. Using the Psalms' parallelisms as our guide, "the saints . . . in whom is all [God's] delight" (Ps. 16:3) include those who are "faithful" (Ps. 31:23) and who "fear" God (Ps. 34:9).

Theological Soundings

IDOLATRY. In the Psalms, idolatry usually refers to the worship of a physical object ("those who pay regard to worthless idols," Ps. 31:6a; see especially Psalm 115:4–7) rather than God ("but I trust in the LORD"; v. 6b). Paul's comments in Colossians 3:5, however, suggest that idolatry can include covetousness, since it is essentially equivalent to worshiping material things.

WORD. The Septuagint[3] Greek of Psalm 33:6—"by the word of the LORD the heavens were made" (ESV)—with the "word" (Greek, *logos*) as the means of creation, probably lies behind John 1:3; the Word came to be seen as a personal agent, one who is both Son of God and God the Son, whom John identifies as Jesus Christ himself (see John 1:14).

Personal Implications

Take time to reflect on the implications of Psalms 32–41 for your own life today. Consider what you have learned that might lead you to praise God, repent of sin, and trust in his gracious promises. Make notes below on the personal implications for your walk with the Lord of the (1) *Gospel Glimpses*, (2) *Whole-Bible Connections*, (3) *Theological Soundings*, and (4) this passage as a whole.

1. Gospel Glimpses

2. Whole-Bible Connections

3. Theological Soundings

4. Psalms 32–41

> ## As You Finish This Unit . . .

Take a moment now to ask for the Lord's blessing and help as you continue in this study of the Psalms. Take a moment also to look back through this unit of study, to reflect on a few key things that the Lord may be teaching you—and perhaps to highlight and underline these things to review again in the future.

Definitions

[1] **Covenant** – A binding agreement between two parties, typically involving a formal statement of their relationship, a list of stipulations and obligations for both parties, a list of witnesses to the agreement, and a list of curses for unfaithfulness and blessings for faithfulness to the agreement.

[2] **My heart** – The phrase "my heart" is used more than 50 times in the Psalter (see "my whole heart"/"their whole heart," used nine times). These phrases express the biblical ideal that the whole inner self should be engaged in loving and praising God (see Deut. 6:5).

[3] **Septuagint** – A Greek translation of the Hebrew Old Testament by Jewish scholars in Alexandria, Egypt, around 200 BC.

WEEK 5: WHY ARE YOU CAST DOWN, O MY SOUL?

Psalms 42–56

▲

The Place of the Passage

The Psalms are not a theology textbook. However, in an unsystematic form they teach us much about topics found in the formal study of systematic theology. In the first half of the second book of the Psalter (Psalms 42–56) we are taught that our souls find rest and salvation in God alone. We move from despair (Ps. 42:1–5) to praise-filled resolution (Ps. 56:10–13).

The Big Picture

Book 2 begins with the first collection of psalms from the Sons of Korah[1] (Psalms 42–49), but once again lament and distress dominate. (For further background, see the *ESV Study Bible*, pages 989–1006, or visit www.esvbible.org.)

Reflection and Discussion

Read through the entire text for this study, Psalms 42–56. Then interact with the following questions concerning this section of the Psalms and record your notes on them.

Because Psalms 42–43 share a refrain, most Bible scholars take them to be a unified lament. Find that refrain. Moreover, both psalms express the longing to return to God's presence in the sanctuary[2] (42:2; 43:3–4). The singer represents himself as separated from temple worship, far from Jerusalem ("the land of Jordan and of Hermon"; 42:5), and subject to the taunts of those who despise his faith. If you read these two psalms as one poem, what is the progression of thought?

It is often difficult to discern if the individual speaker of a psalm speaks for himself or as a representative of all Israel (what is called the "collective I"). Who is the speaker in Psalm 44? Is it a personal lament or a corporate one? What event is described in verse 2? On what basis does the psalmist appeal to God to "awake" (v. 23)?

In the Psalter, what is unique about Psalm 45? Hebrews 1:8–9 cites Psalm 45:6–7. How are those verses used to teach about Christ?

What is the refrain of Psalm 46? How does the refrain summarize the poem's theme?

In Psalm 47, the LORD is called "the King of all the earth" (v. 7) and "the God of Abraham" (v. 9). In Psalm 48 we read about praises in the temple (v. 9) reaching "to the ends of the earth" (v. 10). In Psalm 49, "all the inhabitants of the world" (v. 1) are called to listen. How do those titles and thoughts relate to Genesis 12:1–3 and Matthew 28:19–20?

Many verses from the Psalms have a vertical dimension—i.e., they call God's people to worship God. Other verses have a horizontal dimension—i.e., the congregation calls on one another to believe, say, or do something (see Eph. 5:8–9; Col. 3:16). How does Psalm 48 demonstrate this balance?

In reading the Psalms, we must never forget to ask the question, "What is said about God?" Answer that question for Psalm 50. In light of what is said about God, how are God's covenant people—then and now—to live? How shouldn't we live? Why should we live the way God wants us to?

Psalm 51 is the most famous of the "Penitential Psalms." What specific sin and confrontation was the impetus for writing this psalm? While this psalm is based on a historical situation in David's life, and is thus intensely personal, it also contains instructional elements (see vv. 16–19) and serves as a model for all repentant believers. How so?

The title for Psalm 52 sets the psalm during David's flight from Saul (1 Sam. 21:1–17), which led to the slaughter at Nob of the priests who had helped David (1 Sam. 22:9–19). Doeg's report put the priest's hospitality to David in the worst light (1 Sam. 22:10); when none of Saul's Israelite men would strike the priests down, Doeg willingly did so. He is thus an example of the enemies that the faithful might face. How does that setting shed light on the description of David's ruthless enemies?

Psalm 53 is called a "duplicate psalm" because it is almost identical to Psalm 14 (also compare Psalm 70 with 40:13–17 and Psalm 108 with 57:7–11 and 60:5–12). However, there are differences. What are the differences? What do those differences emphasize?

Some of these Psalms (e.g., Psalm 54) can seem far removed from those of us who are not suffering, especially not suffering religious persecution. How might we be able to pray such psalms *on behalf of* other Christians around the world, many of whom do thus suffer?

We have read plenty of psalms about the godly suffering under the hands of their Gentile enemies. What is unique about *who* harms David in Psalm 55? Any idea whom David has in mind? Have you ever had a painful betrayal? How should you pray during such a sad situation? How can verses 22–23 help? Read also 1 Peter 5:7.

Where is the word "trust" used in Psalm 56? How is the concept of trust expressed in imagery?

Read through the following three sections on *Gospel Glimpses, Whole-Bible Connections,* and *Theological Soundings.* Then take time to consider the *Personal Implications* these sections may have for you.

Gospel Glimpses

GOD'S KINGDOM. As Book 4 concludes with the Psalms' pinnacle of royal theology (Psalm 72), so Psalm 47 sings of the Lord not only as the King of Israel but also as "the King of all the earth" (v. 7). The kingdom of God, of which Jesus so often spoke, is the sovereign rule of God. At the present time, the fallen, sinful world does not belong to the kingdom of God, since it does not submit to God's rule. Instead, God's kingdom can be found in heaven and among his people (Matt. 6:9–10; Luke 17:20–21). When Christ returns, however, the kingdoms of the world will become the kingdom of God (Rev. 11:15). Then all people will, either willingly or regretfully, acknowledge his sovereignty (Phil. 2:9–11). Even the natural world will be transformed to operate in perfect harmony with God (Rom. 8:19–23).

ORIGINAL SIN. This is the condition of both guilt and a propensity to sin, inherited by all people because of their descent from Adam, who committed the first sin. In Psalm 51:5, David assumes this reality: "Behold, I was brought forth [that is, from the womb] in iniquity, and in sin did my mother conceive me." The idea here is not that the act of conception was itself sinful, but (as the parallel first line shows) that each worshiper learns to trace his sinful tendencies to the very beginning of his existence—not only from birth but even from before that, to conception.

However, our original sin (and all sin) is overcome by God's cleansing of sin: "Wash me thoroughly from my iniquity, and cleanse me from my sin!" (v. 2).

"Purge me with hyssop, and I shall be clean; wash me, and I shall be whiter than snow" (v. 7). The terms "wash" and "cleanse" come from the ceremonial system (see Ex. 19:10; Num. 19:19), where they refer to rites that allow a person to come safely into God's presence. Likewise "hyssop" alludes to cleansing ceremonies (Lev. 14:4; Num. 19:18). Such washings point forward to the final cleansing from original (and all!) sin through the work of Christ (Heb. 9:19–28).

Whole-Bible Connections

SACRIFICE. Sacrifices and offerings are mentioned in nearly a dozen psalms, including seven times in Psalms 50–51. Psalm 51:16–17 seems to make temple sacrifices (burnt offerings) relatively unimportant for the faithful, even replacing them with an inner disposition ("a broken and contrite heart"). However, since verse 19 goes on to speak of offering physical sacrifices, it is better to take these verses as implying that the animal sacrifices look to the worshiper offering himself to God as "a living sacrifice" (Rom. 12:1), and without this they lose their significance.

PEACE OFFERINGS. Psalm 50 addresses the right use of sacrifices, focusing on the "sacrifice of thanksgiving" and "vows" (v. 14). These were both kinds of peace offerings (Lev. 7:11–12, 15, 18), which was the only kind of sacrifice in which the worshiper ate some of the sacrificial animal; its primary function was to eat a meal, in company with the sacrificer's family and the needy, with God as the host. First Corinthians 10:16–18 shows that this is the basic meaning of the Christian Lord's Supper.[3]

SUFFERING. Psalm 44:22 describes God's people suffering death at the hands of those who oppose God. In Romans 8:36, Paul uses this verse to remind believers that God's people have always had to face such situations, yet they must not conclude that they are thereby separated from the love of Christ.

Theological Soundings

GOD'S FACE. To enjoy God's presence, or his "face," is the fruition of the covenant (see Ex. 33:14–15; Num. 6:24–26). Like the end of the Bible where we read that we "will see his face" (Rev. 22:4), Psalm 17:15 finishes in triumph, anticipating eternal fellowship in God's presence: In contrast with the wicked, the psalmist writes, "As for me, I shall behold your face in righteousness; when I awake [from the sleep of death], I shall be satisfied with your likeness."

SOUL. Often in the Bible, "soul" describes the life principle that animates the body, or the person's inner self, and can simply be another way of saying "the self." At other times, however, it can describe that inner self as something that survives the death of the body, as it does in Psalm 49:15, where "my soul" is parallel to "me," the believing self that after death will not go to Sheol.[4] In the larger picture of the Bible, the separation of body and soul is unnatural, a product of sin (Gen. 3:19), and it will be healed with their reunion at the resurrection (Dan. 12:2–3; compare 2 Cor. 5:1–4).

GOD'S PEOPLE. Psalm 51 closes by enabling worshipers to see the relationship between their own spiritual health and the well-being of the whole body of God's people (the city of Jerusalem—"Zion"—metaphorically representing God's people in v. 18). That is, each member is linked to all the others in a web of relationships, and together they share in the life of God as it pulses through the whole body. Thus each member contributes to (or detracts from) the health of the whole body. The ideal Israel is a community of forgiven penitents, faithfully embracing God's covenant and worshiping him according to the rites he appointed; this is the community that can bring light to the whole world.

Personal Implications

Take time to reflect on the implications of Psalms 42–56 for your own life today. Consider what you have learned that might lead you to praise God, repent of sin, and trust in his gracious promises. Make notes below on the personal implications for your walk with the Lord of the (1) *Gospel Glimpses*, (2) *Whole-Bible Connections*, (3) *Theological Soundings*, and (4) this passage as a whole.

1. Gospel Glimpses

2. Whole-Bible Connections

3. Theological Soundings

4. Psalms 42–56

> ## As You Finish This Unit . . .

Take a moment now to ask for the Lord's blessing and help as you continue in this study of the Psalms. Take a moment also to look back through this unit of study, to reflect on a few key things that the Lord may be teaching you—and perhaps to highlight and underline these things to review again in the future.

Definitions

[1] **Sons of Korah** – The titles for Psalms 42, 44, 45, 46, 47, 48, and 49 (see also Psalms 84; 85; 87; and 88) mention "the Sons of Korah." They were men from the tribe of Levi who served in the sanctuary (1 Chron. 9:19) as temple musicians (1 Chron. 6:22), and some of them along with Asaph, one of David's appointed choirmasters, were "in charge of the service of song in the house of the Lord" (1 Chron. 6:31).

[2] **Sanctuary** – The tabernacle was the tent where God dwelt on earth and communed with his people as Israel's divine king (also referred to as the "tent of meeting"; Lev. 1:5). The temple in Jerusalem later replaced it. Solomon built the first temple of the Lord in Jerusalem, to replace the portable tabernacle. This temple was later destroyed by the Babylonians, rebuilt, and destroyed again. The inner sanctuary of the tabernacle (and later the temple) was called the Most Holy Place.

[3] **Lord's supper** – A meal of remembrance instituted by Jesus on the night of his betrayal. Christians are to observe this meal, also called Communion, in remembrance of Jesus' death. It consists of the cup, symbolizing the new covenant in his blood, and bread, symbolizing his body, which was broken for his followers.

[4] **Sheol** – Commonly translated "the grave," this Old Testament term predominantly refers to the abode of the dead prior to the coming of Christ. It was associated with descriptions of a dark, prison-like place in the underworld, where the souls of the deceased resided. In the Psalms it sometimes serves as a poetic name for "the grave" or "death" (Ps. 18:5), to which we all go (e.g., Ps. 141:7), and at other times it names the dim destination to which the wicked go but not the faithful (e.g., Ps. 49:14–15).

Week 6: Let the Nations Be Glad

Psalms 57–72

The Place of the Passage

The title for Psalm 72 claims that the author is Solomon. That psalm ends, "Blessed be his glorious name[1] forever; may the whole earth be filled with his glory! Amen and Amen![2] The prayers of David, the son of Jesse, are ended" (vv. 19–20). God's promise to Abraham (Genesis 12) and to David (2 Samuel 7) has begun to be fulfilled. The temple is built and Solomon is on the throne.

The Big Picture

The particular offspring that Abraham, David, and Solomon hoped for was the Messiah—the offspring who will bless all the nations of the earth (Gen. 22:18; Ps. 72:17). (For further background, see the *ESV Study Bible*, pages 1006–1026, or visit www.esvbible.org.)

> ## Reflection and Discussion

Read through the entire text for this study, Psalms 57–72. Then interact with the following questions concerning this section of the Psalms and record your notes on them.

What does the imagery in Psalms 57:4; 58:6–9; and 59:1–7 teach us about David's enemies? While such imagery shows how evil those enemies were, nevertheless, how are Christians to pray verses like 58:10 and 59:12–13? Read Revelation 14:14–20 and 19:1–21.

Shechem, Succoth, Gilead, Manasseh, Ephraim, and Judah were all part of the land that God promised to Israel; while Moab, Edom, and Philistia were neighboring communities (Ps. 60:6–8), which also belonged to the Lord (see Ex. 19:5) and brought great harm to or refused to help God's people. Israel existed to judge the nations but also to bring light to the nations. As Christians, we are not called by God to engage in a holy war for a particular land, and yet like Israel we are to extend God's light to the nations (Matt. 5:14; 28:18–20). What are some ways to faithfully witness to the gospel without being pushovers or allowing injustices?

We have looked at the imagery for David's enemies. Next let's explore imagery used for God and to represent the believer's relationship with him. In Psalms 61:4–5 and 62:2, what are the metaphors for God, and how can these images foster confidence in God, especially when individuals ("O my soul") as well as churches ("O people") are faced with oppression or despair?

There are only 14 historical titles in the Psalms, and eight of them are found in this section (Psalms 51; 52; 54; 56; 57; 59; 60; and 63). However, while those psalms were born out of specific historical situations, note that the psalmists do not pray with historical specifics (e.g., "O Lord, save me from Saul."). This is why such psalms "worked" for public worship in Israel and "work" also today. How can you personally apply Psalm 63 to your life?

Psalms 63 and 64 share many themes. List those themes. What are the three requests given in Psalm 64?

As believers, it is important for us to develop a spirit of gratitude to God. In Psalm 65, how does David express his gratitude? What was the occasion for his gratitude? What are you currently thankful for?

Look at Psalm 66:4 and Psalm 67:3–5. Who does or will worship God? How did that motivate Paul for ministry (read Rom. 15:11)?

The New Testament cites several verses from Psalm 69. Fill out the table below. How do the New Testament writers portray Jesus Christ in light of this psalm?

Psalm 69—what verse?	New Testament	Christ Connection
	John 2:17	
	John 15:25	
	John 19:28–29	
	Acts 1:20	
	Romans 11:9–10	
	Romans 15:3	

Psalm 69:22–28 cries out for God to punish the wicked. What do you think about such petitions for "holy war"? Consult Romans 12:17–21 and Ephesians 6:12.

Psalm 71 is unique in that it speaks of generational praise. What generations are talked about and in what verses?

All but two of the psalms in Psalms 51–72 have in the subscription "to the choir" or "choirmaster." These songs were obviously sung in temple worship. However, these psalms are more than a liturgical library; they are an imprint of public and *personal* experience. Moreover, even psalms that had no named connection with public worship (e.g., Psalm 72) were used for private expression. For example, in Mary's Magnificat (Luke 1:46–55) she weaves together Old Testament Scriptures, including lines from Psalms 72, 98, and 103. Compare Luke 1:46–55 to Psalm 72. What themes are shared?

Read through the following three sections on *Gospel Glimpses*, *Whole-Bible Connections*, and *Theological Soundings*. Then take time to consider the *Personal Implications* these sections may have for you.

Gospel Glimpses

FORGIVE THEM. After Jesus was given sour wine (Ps. 69:21 and John 19:28–29), he felt God-forsaken (Mark 15:34), and the thirst to which he was testifying must have been far more severe and deep-seated than anything this drink was meant for. When Jesus received it, he briefly prolonged his life (and his agony), and perhaps moistened his lips enough finally to cry out, "It is finished!" (John 19:30). In Luke 23:34, Jesus prays, "Father, forgive them, for they know not what they do." Since Luke alluded to Psalm 69, he might well have intended a contrast: the psalm will go on to call down curses on the enemies, while Jesus did not, but instead prayed for mercy. Nevertheless, the judgment requested by the curses is only delayed, and will be set loose when Christ returns as Judge of all.

ACCORDING TO HIS WORK. In Psalm 62:12 we read that the Lord "will render to a man according to his work." This does not teach works righteousness. Rather, a person's "work" shows whether his faith is real or counterfeit. The prospect of a verdict on this should be a ground for confidence for the believer who consciously serves God, and a warning for the unbeliever who does not. At the final judgment, a person's deeds will either vindicate the reality of his faith or reveal the lack thereof (see Matt. 16:27; James 1:12; Rev. 20:13). Moreover, in Romans 2:6 Paul quotes Psalm 62:12 as a judgment on those Jews who rely on their Jewishness rather than on Jesus for their righteousness before God.

Whole-Bible Connections

ALL NATIONS. The last psalm of Book 2 (Psalm 72) is a royal psalm, praying that the heirs of David's line (beginning with Solomon) might have success in the task that God has assigned the king (namely, ruling God's people well, protecting the poor and needy, and bringing blessing to all nations of the earth). Like Psalm 2, this song looks forward to a worldwide rule that embraces in full what the Messiah will accomplish: the Old Testament anticipates the ultimate heir of David, who will take the throne and bring the light of God to all nations (see Isa. 2:1–5; 11:1–10); the New Testament is careful to explain that Jesus, by virtue of his resurrection, has begun to fulfill this task through the Christian mission (see Matt. 28:18–20; Rom. 1:1–6).

SON OF ABRAHAM. The Old Testament very decidedly looks to a future era in which the nations (i.e., "Gentiles") receive God's light. Psalm 67:4–5 is an example of turning the promise to Abraham (Gen. 12:2–3) into song! The earliest Christians announced that in Jesus, "the son of Abraham" (Matt. 1:1), this era has arrived (see Acts 14:17; Rom. 1:1–5, 16).

Theological Soundings

DIVINE ASCENSION. In Ephesians 4:8–11, Paul uses Psalm 68:18 to describe how the exalted Christ (who "ascended" after he descended in the incarnation[3]) distributed gifts to his people. That is, he assigned to each member different ways of serving in the church body. That Paul can apply this verse (about Yahweh) to Christ shows that he considered Jesus divine.

ATONE. Many of the psalms are set in the context of temple worship. For example, Psalm 65 describes acts of public worship at the central sanctuary, such as "praise," "vows," and "prayer." It also speaks of atonement for sins through animal sacrifices: "When iniquities prevail against me, you atone for our transgressions" (v. 3). Only through such atonement could God's people draw near to God and "dwell in" the courts of "the holiness of your temple" (v. 4). Through his death and resurrection, Jesus Christ made atonement for the sins of believers. His death satisfied God's just wrath against sinful humanity, just as Old Testament sacrifices symbolized substitutionary[4] death as payment for sin.

Personal Implications

Take time to reflect on the implications of Psalms 57–72 for your own life today. Consider what you have learned that might lead you to praise God, repent of sin, and trust in his gracious promises. Make notes below on the personal implications for your walk with the Lord of the (1) *Gospel Glimpses*, (2) *Whole-Bible Connections*, (3) *Theological Soundings*, and (4) this passage as a whole.

1. Gospel Glimpses

2. Whole-Bible Connections

3. Theological Soundings

4. Psalms 57–72

As You Finish This Unit . . .

Take a moment now to ask for the Lord's blessing and help as you continue in this study of the Psalms. Take a moment also to look back through this unit of study, to reflect on a few key things that the Lord may be teaching you—and perhaps to highlight and underline these things to review again in the future.

Definitions

[1] **Name** – In the Psalms, the name of the Lord is often the object of religious affections—such as praise, love, trust, and hope (e.g., 5:11; 7:17; 8:1, 9; 18:49; 33:21; 92:1; 96:2; 102:15). Deuteronomy 12:5, 11 speaks of God's "name" dwelling in the sanctuary; i.e., the Lord's name is a way of speaking about his personal presence (see Lev. 19:12; Deut. 6:13) or the sum of his revealed character (Ex. 34:6).

[2] **Amen** – Greek form of a Hebrew word meaning "to confirm." In Scripture and in Christian life, when uttered after a prayer or statement, it means "let it be so."

[3] **Incarnation** – Literally "(becoming) in flesh," it refers to the Son of God becoming a human being without ceasing to be divine, in the person of Jesus of Nazareth.

[4] **Substitutionary** – The idea of "substitutionary atonement" is a way of spelling out the significance of Jesus' death on the cross: Jesus offered himself to die as a substitute for believers. He took upon himself the punishment they deserve and thereby reconciled them to God.

WEEK 7: TRULY GOD
IS GOOD TO ISRAEL

Psalms 73–78

▲

The Place of the Passage

Psalms 73–78 are six of Asaph's 12 psalms in the Psalter. They describe Israel's covenant failures and the consequences—God rebukes and rejects his people. The historical psalm (Psalm 78) summarizes the sad story.

The Big Picture

These psalms show that remembrance of God's past acts of salvation, like the exodus (Ps. 77:19), strengthen the hope for present and future salvation. (For further background, see the *ESV Study Bible*, pages 1026–1037, or visit www. esvbible.org.)

Reflection and Discussion

Read through the entire text for this study, Psalms 73–78. Then interact with the following questions concerning this section of the Psalms and record your notes on them.

Thus far, for each week we have attempted to study a large grouping of psalms. While it is imperative for every week that you read each psalm carefully, the six psalms for this week make that imperative easy to accomplish. Read a psalm a day and take a Sabbath on Sunday! But also, take a day to read them all together in one sitting. As you do so, take notes, prayerfully look for repeated key words and themes, and jot down your own questions. Here is my overview question for you: What do Psalms 73–78 teach you about God's character and concerns? Write a list of specifics below.

What is the psalmist's problem in Psalm 73? How does he vividly describe the people behind his problem (vv. 4–12)? How is the problem resolved?

In the first half of Psalm 74 (vv. 1–11), God seems silent. Why? What has happened? What hasn't God done that the psalmist thought he would do? In the second half (vv. 12–23), he trusts in God. What has changed?

The Psalms were part of Israel's formal worship, and thus they have appropriately been labeled "The Hymnbook of the Old Testament." The psalms were written to be sung. And while they are not doctrinal treatises, they nevertheless teach us much about the content of our lyrics. When you look at a psalm like Psalm 75, what is surprising about its lyrical content? In the church today, we rarely sing lyrics like that. Why not? Should we?

Obviously, the Psalms were written before Jesus Christ was born, crucified, and raised. However, Jesus claims that he is the center of the canon (read Luke 24:25–27, 44). In light of that claim, how should we read Psalm 76?

Find the repeated key words in Psalm 77. How do these words help us arrive at the psalm's theme?

Psalm 78 is a "historical psalm" or a "psalm of remembrance." What are the historical acts recounted? Why are "the glorious deeds of the LORD" (v. 4) recounted? What is the lesson we can learn from this psalm?

Read through the following three sections on *Gospel Glimpses*, *Whole-Bible Connections*, and *Theological Soundings*. Then take time to consider the *Personal Implications* these sections may have for you.

Gospel Glimpses

CUP. In Isaiah 51, the cup represents the cup of God's wrath (Isa. 51:17, 22). Likewise in Jeremiah 25, the cup is "the wine of [God's] wrath" (see Jer. 25:15–28). In Gethsemane, Jesus prayed, "My Father, if it be possible, let this cup pass from me" (Matt. 26:39). To him, the cup signified the culmination of his mission: his awful sufferings and death wherein he would bear in his own body God's judgment upon sin. On the cross, Jesus drank damnation dry!—He "drain[ed] it down to the dregs" (see Ps. 75:7–8).

COVENANT-KEEPING GOD. Psalm 78 is a historical psalm that walks us through several episodes of sin and unbelief, each new section beginning with "they sinned" or "they rebelled" (vv. 17, 32, 40, 56), followed by a final section on God's gift of David as the pinnacle expression of his enduring commitment (vv. 65–72). As Christians, we can see this section on David fulfilled completely in Jesus, David's heir who forever occupies his throne and rules his kingdom. Moreover, we stand amazed in God's patient preservation of the descendants of Abraham—the people into which God has engrafted Gentile Christians. We are the beneficiaries of God's patience!

Whole-Bible Connections

SANCTUARY. In Psalm 73, worshiping God in the sanctuary refocuses the psalmist and renews his faith. In Psalm 74:3, 7, we read that "the enemy has destroyed everything in the sanctuary" and "set your sanctuary on fire . . . bringing it down to the ground," and in Psalm 79:1 we read that "the nations [i.e., Gentiles] . . . have defiled your holy temple [and] laid Jerusalem in ruins." These verses likely refer to the Babylonian destruction of the temple. While in Old Testament times the temple was God's "dwelling place" (Ps. 76:2), nevertheless, even the Old Testament Scriptures are clear that God was never confined to that sacred space (1 Kings 8:27–30; Isa. 66:1–2). Now in Christ—our Immanuel—and through his Holy Spirit who dwells within God's people (Eph. 2:13–22), Christians have permanent access into God's presence, both in this life (John 15:11–16) and in the consummation (Rev. 22:2–4).

EXODUS. Psalms 74 and 77 recount the exodus (see Psalm 105), when under Moses' leadership Israel departed from Egypt and journeyed through the wilderness (Exodus 1–19; Numbers 33). The exodus demonstrated God's power and providence for his people, who had been enslaved by the Egyptians. The annual festival of Passover[1] commemorates God's final plague upon the Egyptians, resulting in Israel's release from Egypt. God's victory in the exodus anticipates Christ's victory over death and Satan (Heb. 2:14–15).

SERVANT. The Lord's "servant" is someone he appointed for a special purpose on behalf of his people (see Ps. 78:70; 89:20; 132:10; 144:10). In the book of Isaiah, the servant of the Lord is never called an heir of David; but the fact that David can be called a servant helps support the messianic interpretation of that figure in Isaiah (i.e., that Jesus is the servant, who rules with justice and mercy but also suffers).

> ## Theological Soundings

COVENANT. A covenant is a binding agreement between two parties, typically involving a formal statement of their relationship, a list of stipulations and obligations for both parties, a list of witnesses to the agreement, and a list of curses for unfaithfulness and blessings for faithfulness to the agreement. The Old Testament is more properly understood as the old covenant, meaning the history of life under the agreement between God and his people prior to the coming of Jesus Christ and the establishment of the new covenant (New Testament). In Psalm 74:20, the psalmist prays to the Lord, "Have regard for the covenant." This refers to God's promise to the patriarchs[2] that was ultimately fulfilled in the new covenant (Heb. 8:8–13).

DARK SAYINGS. Jesus used Psalm 78:2 to describe his own practice of telling parables (Matt. 13:35). He may simply have found this text a convenient summary of what a wisdom teacher does, in order to challenge his audiences to apply themselves to his wisdom; or, he may also have been suggesting that at least some of his parables are like this psalm in drawing lessons from Israel's history (e.g., Matt. 21:33–44).

GRIEVING THE HOLY SPIRIT. In Psalm 78:40, the psalmist speaks of grieving God. There is similar language in Isaiah 63:10, where God's people "rebelled and grieved his Holy Spirit."[3] We Christians can also grieve the Holy Spirit by our sin (Eph. 4:30).

> ## Personal Implications

Take time to reflect on the implications of Psalms 73–78 for your own life today. Consider what you have learned that might lead you to praise God, repent of sin, and trust in his gracious promises. Make notes below on the personal implications for your walk with the Lord of the (1) *Gospel Glimpses*, (2) *Whole-Bible Connections*, (3) *Theological Soundings*, and (4) this passage as a whole.

1. Gospel Glimpses

2. Whole-Bible Connections

3. Theological Soundings

4. Psalms 73–78

As You Finish This Unit . . .

Take a moment now to ask for the Lord's blessing and help as you continue in this study of the Psalms. Take a moment also to look back through this unit of study, to reflect on a few key things that the Lord may be teaching you—and perhaps to highlight and underline these things to review again in the future.

Definitions

[1] **Passover** – An annual Israelite festival meal of roasted lamb commemorating God's final plague on the Egyptians, which opened the door to the exodus. In this final plague, the Lord "passed over" the houses of those who spread the blood of their lamb on the doorposts of their homes (Exodus 12). Those who did not obey this command suffered the death of their firstborn. For Israel, eating the Passover was a celebrating of their redemption.

[2] **Patriarchs** – The earliest ancestors of Israel, primarily Abraham, Isaac, and Jacob.

[3] **Holy Spirit** – The third person of the Trinity, equal in power and glory to the Father and the Son. The Bible mentions several roles of the Holy Spirit, including convicting people of sin, bringing them to conversion, indwelling them and empowering them to live in righteousness and faithfulness, supporting them in times of trial, and enabling them to understand the Scriptures. The Holy Spirit inspired the writers of Scripture, guiding them to record the very words of God. The Holy Spirit was active in the life of Israel's anointed (as noted in the Psalms, e.g., Ps. 51:11; 139:7; 143:10), especially active in Jesus' life and ministry on earth (e.g., Luke 3:22), and is now active in the life of the church and of Christians.

WEEK 8: GLORIFY YOUR NAME

Psalms 79–89

The Place of the Passage

In many ways Books 1 (Psalms 1–41) and 2 (Psalms 42–72) celebrate the golden age of the united monarchy under King David. All the laments end in praise! However, by contrast Book 3 (Psalms 73–89) is covered by a dark, divine (!) shadow. The final lament ends with questions, such as, "Lord, where is your steadfast love of old, which by your faithfulness you swore to David?" (Ps. 89:49).

The Big Picture

Again, the big picture is brighter. We know what God has done in Jesus Christ! Thus, what the psalmist held out in hope ("Blessed be the LORD forever! Amen and Amen"; Ps. 89:52), we now cling to in faith. (For further background, see the *ESV Study Bible*, pages 1037–1052, or visit www.esvbible.org.)

> ## Reflection and Discussion

Read through the entire text for this study, Psalms 79–89. Then interact with the following questions concerning this section of the Psalms and record your notes on them.

The most helpful tip anyone can give you on how to better read, understand, and apply the Psalms is to meditate upon them day and night (Ps. 1:2). Read them. Reread them. Think about them. Ask for the Spirit's illumination. With that in mind, prayerfully read Psalm 79 and list five observations. Circle the one observation that you think is most central to the psalm's main theme.

What is the refrain of Psalm 80? What metaphors are used? How do these images aid the author's message?

Psalm 81 is a "prophetic hymn," which echoes themes found in the Prophets, especially calling the people to covenant faithfulness. Verse 3 refers to the trumpet at the new moon and at the full moon. This may well indicate that the psalm was suited to the Feast of Trumpets (the first day of the seventh month, when the moon was full), with the solemnity of the Day of Atonement[1] to come. Read Leviticus 23:23–36. How does that setting help you understand and apply this psalm?

Psalm 81 also reflects on the exodus[2] and the event at Meribah. Read Exodus 12–14 and 17. How do those events help you understand and apply this psalm?

Read John 10:34–35. How did Jesus use Psalm 82?

Israel used Psalm 83 when they were threatened by Gentile enemies. When and how would Christians use this psalm?

Psalm 84 divides into three parts. The word "blessed" either ends or starts a division. What are the three divisions? How would you summarize the blessing associated with each?

Psalm 84:1–4 uses lofty language about the temple. Why was there such a strong connection in Israel's mind between God's house and God himself? Since Jesus is now the temple (Immanuel—"God with us," Matt. 1:23; compare John 2:21), how would you translate verses like verses 1–4 into the appropriate language for Christian worship?

In Luke 11:1, the disciples ask Jesus, "Lord, teach us to pray." Jesus replied with the Lord's Prayer. How do Psalms 85–86 aid your prayer life? That is, how do they teach Christians how to pray and what to pray for?

What are the questions asked of God in Psalm 88?

How many times are "steadfast love" and "faithfulness" mentioned in Psalm 89? Yet, what is the problem?

_____

_____

_____

_____

_____

_____

A covenant is a binding agreement between two parties, typically involving a formal statement of their relationship, a list of stipulations and obligations for both parties, a list of witnesses to the agreement, and a list of curses for unfaithfulness and blessings for faithfulness to the agreement. The concept of covenant is a major theme in the Old Testament. Twelve psalms focus on God's covenant with his people, notably Psalm 89. What does this psalm teach about God's covenant relationship with Israel? How does this psalm anticipate the coming of Jesus and the new covenant (see Matt. 1:12–16; Luke 3:23–38)?

_____

_____

_____

_____

_____

_____

Read through the following three sections on _Gospel Glimpses_, _Whole-Bible Connections_, and _Theological Soundings_. Then take time to consider the _Personal Implications_ these sections may have for you.

Gospel Glimpses

ATONEMENT. Throughout the Old Testament, it takes a sacrifice to make atonement for sins. In Psalm 79:9, however, the temple is no more (v. 1), and yet the psalmist asks God to "atone for our sins." This shows that God's hands were not tied to the sacrificial system. Moreover, it prefigures the forgiveness offered to us in Jesus' death.

MYSTERY. Psalm 87:4–6 is shocking! From an Old Testament context, it is shocking because various Gentile nations—Rahab (a nickname for Egypt; see Isa. 30:7), Babylon, Philistia, Tyre, and Cush—are described as "those who know" the Lord. How is it that "the Most High himself will establish" Zion in a way that includes these Gentiles, all of whom had been, at one time or another, enemies of God's people and city? In Ephesians, the apostle Paul called the inclusion of Gentile sinners into the people of God "the mystery of the gospel" (6:19; see 1:9; 3:3–10).

Whole-Bible Connections

SON. In the Old Testament (e.g., Ex. 4:22–23; Hos. 11:1), including the Psalms (e.g., Ps. 80:15), Israel as a whole is called God's "son." Psalm 80:16–18 also adds the term "the son of man"[3] (also, "the man of your right hand"). One reason New Testament writers call Jesus God's Son and the Son of Man is to show that he embodies all that Israel was called to be but was not. In his faithfulness, God through Christ has restored and saved his people (Ps. 80:19).

GLORY. The "glory" mentioned, for example, in Psalm 85:9, is God's special presence with his people. From the verb "dwell" (in Hebrew, *skakan*) is derived the noun, "dwelling, that which dwells" (Hebrew, *shekinah*), which is why the glory that dwells with God's people in the sanctuary is sometimes referred to as the "Shekinah." This dwelling of the glory is a gift to God's people, and it was ultimately expressed in the incarnation: "And the Word became flesh and *dwelt* among us, and we have seen his *glory*, *glory* as of the only Son from the Father, full of grace and truth" (John 1:14).

Theological Soundings

WORSHIP. In Psalm 86:8, the psalmist moves from "there is none like you among the gods"[4] (i.e., the angels, other heavenly beings, or human kings), to "God" who alone is worthy of worship (v. 10). As promised to Abraham (Gen. 12:3), here the psalmist prophesies that "all the nations" will worship "the Lord" as the one true God. According to the New Testament, the era described here has begun with the resurrection of Jesus, the Lamb of God (see Rev. 15:4).

GOD'S JEALOUSY. The notion of God being "jealous" involves the use of ana-logical language to describe the "marriage" relationship between God and his people (see "hold fast" in Gen. 2:24; Deut. 10:20). Unlike human jealousy, which can be irrational (see Num. 5:14), God has a passionate commitment to receiving exclusive loyalty from his people—a commitment for their good. If God's people are unfaithful, God's jealousy "burn[s] like fire" (Ps. 79:5).

FIRSTBORN. Just as Israel is God's "firstborn" (Ex. 4:22), so the Davidic king (Ps. 89:26–28) is the firstborn as the people's embodiment. The New Testament calls Jesus the "firstborn," portraying him as the exalted heir of David who represents his people (Rom. 8:29; Col. 1:15, 18; Heb. 1:6; Rev. 1:5). He is the one who fulfills the prospect of being "the highest of the kings of the earth" (Ps. 89:27; compare Rev. 1:5; 19:16; Matt. 28:18–19).

Personal Implications

Take time to reflect on the implications of Psalms 79–89 for your own life today. Consider what you have learned that might lead you to praise God, repent of sin, and trust in his gracious promises. Make notes below on the personal implications for your walk with the Lord of the (1) *Gospel Glimpses*, (2) *Whole-Bible Connections*, (3) *Theological Soundings*, and (4) this passage as a whole.

1. Gospel Glimpses

2. Whole-Bible Connections

3. Theological Soundings

4. Psalms 79–89

> ## As You Finish This Unit . . .

Take a moment now to ask for the Lord's blessing and help as you continue in this study of the Psalms. Take a moment also to look back through this unit of study, to reflect on a few key things that the Lord may be teaching you—and perhaps to highlight and underline these things to review again in the future.

Definitions

[1] **Day of Atonement** – The holiest day in the Israelite calendar, when atonement was made for all the sins of Israel from the past year (Leviticus 16). It occurred on the tenth day of the seventh month (September/October), and all Israel was to fast and refrain from work. Only on that day each year could someone—the high priest—enter the Most Holy Place of the tabernacle (later, the temple) and offer the necessary sacrifices. A "scapegoat" would also be sent into the wilderness as a sign of Israel's sins being carried away.

[2] **Exodus** – The departure of the people of Israel from Egypt and their journey to Mount Sinai under Moses' leadership (Exodus 1–19). The exodus demonstrated God's power and providence for his people, who had been enslaved by the Egyptians. The annual festival of Passover commemorates God's final plague upon the Egyptians, resulting in Israel's release from Egypt.

[3] **Son of man** – The title Jesus uses more than any other to refer to himself (e.g., Matt. 8:20; 11:19). While labeling himself this way may underscore Jesus' humanity, the phrase is most significant in relation to the figure in Daniel 7 who receives supreme authority and an everlasting kingdom from God (compare Dan. 7:13–14 and Matt. 26:64).

[4] **Gods** – The term "gods" or "mighty lords" (e.g., Ps. 58:1) can refer to human rulers who wield their might by God's appointment (Ps. 82:1; 138:1; compare Ex. 15:15; Job 41:25). It is certainly humans Jesus was referring to when he quoted Psalm 82:6 in a debate to deflect criticism for calling himself the "Son of God" (John 10:34–36).

WEEK 9: MY FOOT SLIPS

Psalms 90–106

▲

The Place of the Passage

Psalms 90–106 comprise Book 4 of the Psalms. While Moses is mentioned seven times in this section of the Psalms, once again God is held up as Israel's ultimate Savior—past, present, and future. God remembers his covenant and sustains the faithful.

The Big Picture

Psalms 93–99 are called "enthronement psalms" because they look to the Lord's final reign on earth, culminating in the kingdom rule of Jesus Christ (Heb. 1:10–12, quoting Ps. 102:25–27). (For further background, see the *ESV Study Bible*, pages 1052–1078, or visit www.esvbible.org.)

Reflection and Discussion

Read through the entire text for this study, Psalms 90–106. Then interact with the following questions concerning this section of the Psalms and record your notes on them.

Psalm 91 is a tender and intimate psalm that describes the confidence that the believer may have through all manner of dangers and challenges. Look at verses 3–8. What are the benefits that come to those who trust in the Lord? When Jesus was tempted in the wilderness, the Devil quoted Psalm 91:11–12 (Matt. 4:6). How did the Devil use those verses? How did Jesus respond in trust (Matt. 4:1–11)?

Some of the psalms were written for and/or were intended to be sung during particular festivals or celebrations (e.g., Psalm 65 as a harvest thanksgiving). In addition to the festivals, certain psalms (e.g., Psalm 92) were written for the weekly Sabbath worship, as a day of "holy convocation" (Lev. 23:3). How does that context shed light on the themes of Psalm 92?

Some of the psalms share "affinity groupings." For example, Psalm 93 along with Psalms 95–99 can be grouped under the heading of "psalms celebrating God's universal kingship." In one short phrase, how does Psalm 93 express God's kingship?

There are pitfalls we must be aware of when reading the Psalms as Christians. The first pitfall is that we would ignore a psalm's original setting; the second is that we would limit the application to only the original audience. What verses in Psalm 94 are used in Romans 11:2, 1 Corinthians 3:20, and Hebrews 12:5–6, and how?

In the contemporary church, verses 1–7a of Psalm 95 are often used as a call to worship, while verses 7b–11 are ignored. Why might this be the case? Read Hebrews 3:7–11. Which half of the psalm does the author of Hebrews use to call the church to continue to worship? Why?

Psalm 96 has three sections, each beginning with a command and each mentioning the Gentiles. Find the commands and list the references to Gentiles. What was Israel's view of their mission in the world (see Psalm 98)?

God wins! Psalm 97 is a hymn that celebrates God's rule over creation, focusing on how God's universal rule assures the faithful of his final victory over evil and idolatry.[1] That theme looks forward to the reign of Jesus Christ (read the book of Revelation). However, its language also echoes praises from the Pentateuch, especially the book of Exodus. See how this is the case. Below, fill in the similar phrases:

Psalms	Exodus	Similar Phrase
Psalm 97:1	Exodus 15:18	
Psalm 97:2–5	Exodus 19:9, 16, 18	
Psalm 97:6	Exodus 16:7	
Psalm 97:9	Exodus 15:11	

In Psalm 98:1, we are exhorted, "Oh sing to the LORD a new song,[2] for he has done marvelous things!" In Revelation 5:9 another "new song" is sung to Jesus in celebration of what he has done for the world. What mighty acts of salvation would the first singers of Psalm 98 recount in their worship? As Christians, what acts of salvation can we add to those?

Psalm 99 is a beautiful example of what is taught throughout the Psalter—that the Lord is both transcendent and immanent. How does this psalm blend those seemingly paradoxical attributes?

In Hebrews 1, the author cites a number of Old Testament texts to show that Jesus is superior to angelic beings. Look at Hebrews 1:10. What verses from Psalm 102 does he quote to support his argument? What does that quotation teach you about the deity of Christ?

Psalm 103:17–18 connects faith (the fear of the Lord) with obedience (keeping the covenant). Other psalms stress that same point (e.g., Ps. 105:45; 112:1, 7; compare 2:11). Where else in Psalm 103 is that connection made? Read John 14:15, 21; 15:10. How does Jesus make the same connection?

Psalms 104–106 recall the storyline from creation to the exile.[3] Read through these psalms and write down the major events mentioned in Israel's history. As a Christian, if you were to write a psalm, what acts in salvation history would you add after Israel's exile?

Read through the following three sections on *Gospel Glimpses*, *Whole-Bible Connections*, and *Theological Soundings*. Then take time to consider the *Personal Implications* these sections may have for you.

Gospel Glimpses

HOLY IS HE. In Psalm 99, we read, "the LORD our God is holy" (v. 9), and, "Holy is he!" (vv. 3, 5). That psalm also exults in God's forgiveness (v. 8). In the Old Testament, through the temple sacrifices and priests,[4] God graciously made a way to come into his presence. In the New Testament, we come to God through Jesus Christ.

HEALS. This word is often used to refer to curing someone from a physical sickness. However, it can also be used as a metaphor for restoring the moral and spiritual life (e.g., Isa. 6:10; 53:5). This is the sense in Psalm 103, where "heals" is parallel with "forgives," and "diseases" with "iniquity." This is similar to how Matthew uses Isaiah 53:5—to look beyond the Servant's healing ministry to the cross (Matt. 8:16–17).

Whole-Bible Connections

SABBATH. Saturday, the seventh day of the week, the Jewish day of worship and rest (Gen. 2:2–3; Ex. 31:13–17; Lev. 23:3). Christians meet for worship on Sunday, the day of Christ's resurrection (Acts 20:7), and regard Sunday, rather than Saturday, as their weekly day of rest. And yet, every day, believers look forward to our eternal Sabbath rest (Heb. 4:1–13).

WORSHIP HIM. Hebrews 1:6 quotes Psalm 97:7—a text about God—and applies it to Jesus. The New Testament recognizes that Jesus was the God of Israel in human flesh (see John 1:14).

FATHER. In Psalm 103:13 God's steadfast love is compared to a "father [who] shows compassion to his children." In the New Testament Jesus calls God "my Father" (Matt. 7:21) and teaches his disciples to call God "Father" (6:9).

Theological Soundings

GOD OF VENGEANCE. The notion of vengeance is founded on God's justice: he brings his righteous judgment on those who oppose him and harm his people (see Deut. 32:35, 41, 43; Ps. 18:47; 94:1). While one function of the civil government is to ensure just vengeance against wrongdoers (Ex. 21:20; compare Rom. 13:4), the Bible forbids individuals to take vengeance into their own hands (Lev. 19:18; compare Rom. 12:19). God will carry out vengeance against those who despise him (2 Thess. 1:8), and the faithful will rejoice because God's justice has been vindicated (Ps. 58:10; 79:10; Rev. 6:10).

THE WHOLE WORLD WORSHIPS. When all kinds of people gladly receive God's rule, worshiping him according to his gracious character, the rest of creation ("the heavens . . . the earth . . . the sea," and "the field" with all their inhabitants, and "the trees of the forest") will all celebrate ("be glad . . . rejoice . . . roar . . . exult" and "sing for joy"; Ps. 96:10–13). The creation suffers from the curse upon humankind, God's discipline of wayward humans, and the evil that people do; but when they genuinely come under the rule of the true God, the blessings will spread throughout the world (Rom. 8:18–25).

SAINTS. In both the Old and New Testaments, this term refers not to *especially holy people* but to God's people, who strive for holiness by means of God's power and so honor their commitment to his covenant. In Psalm 97, the term parallels those "who love the Lord" (v. 10), the "righteous" (vv. 11, 12), and the "upright in heart" (v. 11).

Personal Implications

Take time to reflect on the implications of Psalms 90–106 for your own life today. Consider what you have learned that might lead you to praise God, repent of sin, and trust in his gracious promises. Make notes below on the personal implications for your walk with the Lord of the (1) *Gospel Glimpses*, (2) *Whole-Bible Connections*, (3) *Theological Soundings*, and (4) this passage as a whole.

1. Gospel Glimpses

2. Whole-Bible Connections

3. Theological Soundings

4. Psalms 90–106

As You Finish This Unit . . .

Take a moment now to ask for the Lord's blessing and help as you continue in this study of the Psalms. Take a moment also to look back through this unit of study, to reflect on a few key things that the Lord may be teaching you—and perhaps to highlight and underline these things to review again in the future.

Definitions

[1] **Idolatry** – In the Bible, idolatry usually refers to the worship of a physical object. Paul's comments in Colossians 3:5, however, suggest that idolatry can include covetousness, since it is essentially equivalent to worshiping material things.

[2] **New song** – This term (see Ps. 33:3; 40:3; 96:1; 98:1; 144:9; 149:1; Isa. 42:10; Rev. 5:9; 14:3) need not imply a freshly composed song; instead it may mean singing this song as a response to a fresh experience or demonstration of God's grace.

[3] **Exile** – Typically refers to the Babylonian exile, that is, Nebuchadnezzar's relocation of residents of the southern kingdom of Judah to Babylon in 586 BC. (Residents of the northern kingdom of Israel had been resettled by Assyria in 722 BC.) After Babylon came under Persian rule, several waves of Jewish exiles returned and repopulated Judah.

[4] **Priest** – In Old Testament Israel, the priest represented the people before God and God before the people. Only those descended from Aaron could be priests. Their prescribed duties also included inspecting and receiving sacrifices from the people and overseeing the daily activities and maintenance of the tabernacle or temple.

WEEK 10: I WILL
AWAKE THE DAWN!

Psalms 107–119

The Place of the Passage

Psalms 107–150 comprise Book 5 of the Psalms, and they celebrate God's stead-fast love (107:1; 108:1; 117:2; 118:1). These psalms begin by praising God for gathering exiled Israel (Ps. 107:1–3) and conclude with a call for all creation to praise the Lord (Ps. 150:6).

The Big Picture

Israel's long exile is over with the coming of Christ, whose predicted reign through his death and resurrection is foretold in Psalm 110. (For further back-ground, see the *ESV Study Bible*, pages 1078–1102, or visit www.esvbible.org.)

> ## Reflection and Discussion

Read through the entire text for this study, Psalms 107–119. Then interact with the following questions concerning this section of the Psalms and record your notes on them.

Psalm 107 expresses the tribe of Judah's gratitude to God for their return from exile. Notice the word "some." It designates four different groups. Summarize what is said about each group during the exile.

In the Psalms God is praised for his mighty acts in history, the stunning majesty of creation, personal and corporate rescue from enemies, and for his written revelation. In Psalm 108, for what in particular is God praised?

In Psalm 109 the psalmist is persecuted. Thus, he gives himself to prayer (v. 4). What does he pray for (vv. 6–20)? Why does he pray in this way—what has the wicked man done? How did the earliest Christians apply this psalm (see Acts 1:20)?

Psalm 110 is quoted more than any other psalm in the New Testament. Read where and how it is quoted—Matthew 22:44–45 (see also Mark 12:35–37; Luke 20:41–44; Acts 2:34–36; 1 Cor. 15:25–28; Eph. 1:22; Heb. 1:13; 5:6; 7:17, 21). Summarize the two main truths taught about Jesus in those texts.

Both Psalm 111 and 112 follow an acrostic pattern (after "Praise the Lord," the first word of each line begins with the successive letter of the Hebrew alphabet), and therefore these psalms illuminate each other. What does Psalm 111 say about "the LORD"? What does Psalm 112 say about "the man who fears the LORD"?

Psalms 113–118 are often called the "Egyptian Hallel" psalms (more on that below). Read them together. What themes do they share?

Read 1 Samuel 2:1–11—Hannah's song of praise for God's answer to her petition for a son. Read also Luke 1:46–53, Mary's Magnificat. Now, read Psalm 113. What similarities do you see? What do those similarities express to you?

What historical events in Israel's history are alluded to in Psalm 114? The psalm uses exuberant personification (a figure of speech in which something nonhuman is given human attributes) to describe some of these events. Give an example or two.

Psalm 115 gives a picture of Israel's God versus the nations' idols. What is said about God? What is said about idols (see Isa. 44:9–20)? How does such satire help you "trust in the LORD"?

Psalm 116 is a very personal psalm of thanksgiving for God's care. How can this psalm help you grow in your "love" (v. 1) for the Lord? Read Romans 3:3 and 2 Corinthians 4:13. How did Paul apply verses from this psalm?

How, in Hebrews 13:6, is Psalm 118:6 applied to Jewish Christians? How did various New Testament authors (Matt. 21:42; Mark 12:10–11; Luke 20:17; Acts 4:11; 1 Pet. 2:7) apply Psalm 118:22–23?

There are short Psalms (Psalm 117) and long ones (Psalm 119). Psalm 119 is the longest psalm and the longest "chapter" in the Bible! Psalm 119 is a hymn about the Bible. (It is also an acrostic poem—there are 22 stanzas of eight verses each; all eight verses start with one of the 22 letters of the Hebrew alphabet.) It uses synonyms for God's written revelation. What are those synonyms? What are the psalmist's attitudes and actions in relation to each word?

Read through the following three sections on *Gospel Glimpses*, *Whole-Bible Connections*, and *Theological Soundings*. Then take time to consider the *Personal Implications* these sections may have for you.

Gospel Glimpses

ORDER OF MELCHIZEDEK. Psalm 110:4 says of the Messiah, "You are a priest forever after the order of Melchizedek." Melchizedek was "king of Salem" (Jerusalem) and a "priest of God Most High"[1] (Gen. 14:18–20) who met Abraham after a battle, blessed him, and received a tenth of his spoils. The author of Hebrews reveals that Jesus is this king/priest (Heb. 5:6) whose sin offering—himself!—atoned for our sins.

OUT FROM EGYPT. The crossing of the Red Sea (Exodus 14–15) and the Jordan River (Joshua 3), two events described briefly in Psalm 114:3, are acts of salvation and symbolic triumphs over death that anticipate the triumph of Christ (John 10:18; 11:25; Rev. 1:18; 21:4).

Whole-Bible Connections

EGYPTIAN HALLEL PSALMS. Psalms 113–118 are often called the "Egyptian Hallel" psalms ("Egyptian" because of their later connection with the Passover, and "Hallel" because of the theme of "praise" [*hallel* in Hebrew]). In later times, the final psalm (Psalm 118) was sung at the Feast of Tabernacles as well as at Passover. It was recited by the crowds when Jesus entered Jerusalem on Palm Sunday—"Hosanna[2] to the Son of David! Blessed is he who comes in the name of the Lord! Hosanna in the highest!" (Matt. 21:9)—and it was likely the "hymn" that Jesus and his disciples sang after their Passover meal (26:30). Perhaps it will be sung again at Christ's second coming (see 23:39)!

CALLING OF THE GENTILES. The shortest psalm in the Psalter touches on one of the grandest themes in the Bible. Psalm 117 invites all nations to "praise the LORD." While the Lord's "steadfast love" and "faithfulness" are toward Israel, the calling of Israel was for the sake of the whole world (Gen. 12:2–3; Ex. 19:5–6; 1 Kings 8:41–43), and the Old Testament constantly nurtures the hope that a day will come when the Gentiles will gladly join in worshiping the one true God. As part of his argument for Jewish and Gentile Christians welcoming one another and worshiping together, Paul quotes Psalm 117:1 in Romans 15:11. That time has arrived!

Theological Soundings

FEAR OF THE LORD. Fear has both godly and ungodly meanings in the Bible, depending on the context. Jesus taught his disciples not to fear people or situations in a way that shows lack of trust in God's protection (Matt. 10:26–31). The fear of the Lord, however, is a godly, wise fear that demonstrates awe and reverence for the all-powerful God (Prov. 1:7). In the Psalms, this fear involves trust and obedience (Ps. 112:1, 7; compare, those who have "no fear of God," Ps. 36:1; quoted by Paul in Rom. 3:18 as part of Paul's charge that both Jews and Gentiles are under sin).

CHARACTER AND COMMUNITY. Certain psalms, like Psalm 112, focus on the moral character of the godly person and the benefits of righteous living. In 2 Corinthians 9:9, Paul quotes Psalm 112:9, encouraging mostly Gentile Christians to give generously to the poor Jewish church in Judea. There is an ethical connection between Christians who trust in the Lord (Ps. 112:7) and sacrificial distribution to the poor (v. 9).[3]

Personal Implications

Take time to reflect on the implications of Psalms 107–119 for your own life today. Consider what you have learned that might lead you to praise God, repent of sin, and trust in his gracious promises. Make notes below on the personal implications for your walk with the Lord of the (1) *Gospel Glimpses*, (2) *Whole-Bible Connections*, (3) *Theological Soundings*, and (4) this passage as a whole.

1. Gospel Glimpses

2. Whole-Bible Connections

3. Theological Soundings

4. Psalms 107–119

As You Finish This Unit . . .

Take a moment now to ask for the Lord's blessing and help as you continue in this study of the Psalms. Take a moment also to look back through this unit of study, to reflect on a few key things that the Lord may be teaching you—and perhaps to highlight and underline these things to review again in the future.

Definitions

[1] **Most high** – Often used of God throughout the Psalms to express that the Lord is exalted above every earthly and heavenly power.

[2] **Hosanna** – The expression "save us, we pray" (e.g., Ps. 118:25), when transliterated into Greek, became *hōsanna* (see Matt. 21:9, 15; Mark 11:9, 10; John 12:13).

[3] **The poor** – This term usually refers to the oppressed or exploited (financially or otherwise) among God's people.

WEEK 11: THE SONGS OF ASCENTS

Psalms 120–134

▲

The Place of the Passage

Psalms 120–134 are called the Songs of Ascents. While likely composed on various occasions and for various purposes, these 15 psalms were later grouped together and sung by pilgrims as they *ascended* (walked uphill) to Jerusalem to worship the Lord (Ps. 122:4).

The Big Picture

While these psalms have diverse authors (including David) and include nearly all the categories of psalms (including lament, wisdom, and thanksgiving), the themes of God's people rejoicing in or near God's place (the temple)[1] over the steadfast love, forgiveness, and promised peace of God are consistent. (For further background, see the *ESV Study Bible*, pages 1102–1111, or visit www .esvbible.org).

Reflection and Discussion

Read through Psalms 120–134, the passage for this week's study. Then review the following questions, taking notes.

It is always important to remember that the Psalms are God-centered prayers/songs. Read Psalms 120–134 with this in mind. How many times is "the LORD" mentioned? (Count the pronouns too!) List all the Lord's actions—what he did, does, and will do.

Throughout these psalms, the psalmists openly share with the Lord their needs and desires. *How* do they make requests and *what* do they ask for? Follow-up: how does what they do instruct your own prayer life?

Psalm 121 is a psalm of protection. What repeated phrase emphasizes this theme?

In Psalm 126, what phrase is repeated three times? Why should Israel act with that emotion? Put simply, what reasons are given for rejoicing?

Psalms 127 and 128 mention the blessing of children. What are the specific blessings? Do they still apply today? If not, why not? If so, how so?

In Psalm 125:4, the psalmist speaks of "those who are good" and how God rewards the righteous. However, in Psalm 130:3, the psalmist writes, "If you, O LORD, should mark iniquities, O Lord, who could stand?" How do you reconcile those two seemingly contradictory ideas?

What are the different words used to express faith in Psalms 125, 128, and 130? What are the images used in Psalms 130 and 131?

Read 2 Samuel 7. How does this help our understanding of Psalm 132? Of these 15 psalms, only Psalm 132 is quoted and/or alluded to in the New Testament. Compare Psalm 132:5 with Acts 7:46; Psalm 132:11 with Acts 2:30; and Psalm 132:17 with Luke 1:69. What light do those New Testament texts shed on this Old Testament psalm?

What is the central theme of Psalm 133? What two images are used to explain that theme? How do those images help explain the theme? Around whom and

what is Israel united? Around whom and what is the church united? Consider
Ephesians 4:1–6.

There are two psalms that call for God's people to respond—"let Israel[2] now
say." What are those two psalms? What might be the purpose of such a structure?

God's blessing and judgment are prominent themes in these psalms, as we
have seen in earlier ones. Whom does God bless, and why? Whom does God
judge, and why?

Read through the following three sections on *Gospel Glimpses, Whole-Bible
Connections,* and *Theological Soundings*. Then take time to consider the *Personal
Implications* these sections may have for you.

Gospel Glimpses

PEACE. While the psalmists repeatedly ask God for military peace in Jerusalem
for Israel (e.g., Ps. 120:6, 7; 122:6, 7, 8; 125:5; 128:6), we know that through
Jesus Christ both Jews and Gentiles are offered spiritual peace with God and
each other (Eph. 4:3; Col. 3:15). We also long for the return of the Prince of
Peace on the last day, when God's people will experience true and final peace.

FORGIVENESS OF SIN. Sin is any violation of or failure to adhere to the commands of God, or the desire to go astray. Forgiveness is the release from guilt and
the reestablishment of a harmonious relationship. Forgiveness can be granted
by God to human beings (Luke 24:47; Acts 2:38; Col. 1:13–14; 1 John 1:9) and
by human beings to those who have wronged them (Matt. 18:21–22; Col. 3:13).

Whole-Bible Connections

JERUSALEM. Jerusalem (also called "Mount Zion" and "Zion") is mentioned 12 times in these 15 psalms and alluded to a number of other times throughout the Psalter. Israel's holy city prefigures the heavenly Jerusalem (Gal. 4:26), the place where through Jesus, "the mediator of a new covenant," we gather to worship the living God (Heb. 12:22–24).

JOY. Just as the psalmists often experienced joy in the presence of God in the temple (e.g., Ps. 122:1; compare 27:4), so Christians are given the joy of knowing God in Christ (John 15:11; 16:24; 17:3), which is to be fulfilled in the consummation (Rev. 19:6–9; 22:4).

DAVID. God's covenant with David (2 Sam. 7:4–16) is alluded to throughout Psalm 132. In verses 11–12 specifically, the psalmist's trust reminds Israel (and earlier God!—"Remember, O LORD, in David's favor"; v. 1) of God's promise of an heir to sit upon David's throne forever. We know that Jesus, the Son of David, is the fulfillment of that promise (Matt. 1:1–16; Acts 2:30–32).

Theological Soundings

CREATOR. While worshiping the Lord in Jerusalem is a focus of the Songs of Ascents—"Let us go to the house of the LORD!" (Ps. 122:1), nevertheless, we repeatedly read of God as Creator—"who made heaven and earth" (Ps. 121:2; 124:8; 134:3).

TEMPLE. In the Old Testament, the temple was the place where God's faithful presence and forgiving power were "housed." However, even in the Songs of Ascents—where Jerusalem's temple is much in focus—we read that God is "enthroned in the heavens" (Ps. 123.1; see Acts 7:48), not merely in Jerusalem's temple. Such knowledge anticipates Jesus' replacing the temple (Matt. 12:6; 24:2; 26:61; 27:40, 51). Jesus is Immanuel (Matt. 1:23; compare John 1:14), the one and only place/person where God's saving presence is now found. Through his death, resurrection, and ascension,[3] we have a perfect and permanent sacrifice and intercessor for our sins (Heb. 7:23–28), as well as the gift of the Spirit who dwells within all (Eph. 2:13–22) who worship God in Spirit and in truth (John 4:23–24).

Personal Implications

Take time to reflect on the implications of Psalms 120–134 for your own life today. Make notes below on the personal implications for your walk with the Lord of the (1) *Gospel Glimpses*, (2) *Whole-Bible Connections*, (3) *Theological Soundings*, and (4) these Psalms as a whole.

1. Gospel Glimpses

2. Whole-Bible Connections

3. Theological Soundings

4. Psalms 120–134

As You Finish This Unit . . .

Take a moment now to ask for the Lord's blessing and help as you continue in this study of the Psalms. Take a moment also to look back through this unit of study, to reflect on a few key things that the Lord may be teaching you—and perhaps to highlight or underline to review again in the future.

Definitions

[1] **Temple** – There are many names used for the temple in the Psalms (house, tent, sanctuary, etc.). In the Old Testament, the temple is the place where God "sits enthroned" (Ps. 9:11; 22:3; 1 Sam. 4:4; 2 Sam. 6:2) as king forever, especially over his people.

[2] **Israel** – Originally, another name given to Jacob (Gen. 32:28). Later applied to the nation formed by his descendants, then to the 10 northern tribes of that nation, who rejected the anointed king and formed their own nation. In the New Testament, the name is applied to the church as the spiritual descendants of Abraham (Gal. 6:16).

[3] **Ascension** – The departure of the resurrected Jesus to God the Father in heaven (Luke 24:50–51; Acts 1:1–12).

WEEK 12:
LET EVERYTHING
THAT HAS BREATH

Psalms 135–150

The Place of the Passage

As the book of Psalms moves us through David's struggles with Saul (Psalms 3–41) and kingly reign (Psalms 42–72), past the Assyrian conflict (Psalms 73–89) and destruction of the temple (Psalms 90–106), so it ends with reflections on return from exile (Psalms 107–145) and calls for all creation to worship the Lord of the covenant (Psalms 146–150).

The Big Picture of Psalms

While in the Psalms there are more "laments" than "hymns of praise," the Psalter ends with an explosion of praise—with the five "hallelujah hymns" (Psalms 146–150)! We can see why in Hebrew the book is entitled *tehillim* ("songs of praise"). (For further background, see the *ESV Study Bible*, pages 1111–1128, or visit www.esvbible.org.)

Reflection and Discussion

Read through the entire text for this study, Psalms 135–150. Then interact with the following questions concerning this section of the Psalms and record your notes on them.

In Psalm 135 God is labeled "good" and "great." Why? Compare his person and works with other "gods."

Psalm 136 expands upon the themes of Psalm 135. Note the inclusio[1] (vv. 1, 26). Note also the obvious refrain in *every* verse. List God's "great wonders" for which Israel is to give thanks. What are the three main historical events described? Also read Psalm 138, another psalm of thanks. For what does David give thanks?

Psalm 137 ends with a ferocious curse! What is it? How can the context of the psalm shed light on that curse (vv. 1–6)? How can prophecies like Isaiah 13:16, 19; 47:1–9; Jer. 50:46; 51:24 help us understand this prayer? Put differently, how does this curse accord with divine revelation—"to execute on them the judgment written" (Ps. 149:9)?

Psalms 138–145 are the final collection of psalms attributed to David. Psalm 139 is the most popular of this collection. Its popularity is due in part to its theme of God's intimate knowledge of his people (note the verb "know"; vv. 1, 2, 4, 6, 23) and the beautiful language used to express that theme (e.g., "you knitted me together in my mother's womb"; v. 13). However, read verses 19–22. What is surprising about these verses? How do you make sense of them in light of the rest of the psalm? Note also the immediate context. Read Psalms 137, 140, and 143:2 (see also Psalms 5; 54, 56; 59; 69; 70; 71; and 109).

Read 1 Samuel 24:1–17 (see 22:1). Then read Psalm 142 (see Psalm 57). How does the historical context shape your reading of the psalm?

Some of the psalmists accept their situation quietly, while others show their exasperation by questioning God (e.g., Psalm 142). Is it right to talk this way to God—to "pour out [our] complaint before him"?

How does the confidence in answered prayer displayed in Psalm 143:12 relate to the petition in verse 11?

Psalms 135 and 150 start "Praise the LORD."[2] Similarly, Psalms 135, 146, 147, 148, 149, and 150 begin and end with "Praise the LORD." All six verses of Psalm 150 contain the imperative "praise"! Read those psalms together. List at least three reasons given for such exuberant worship.

While there is a Psalms scroll from the Dead Sea Scrolls that attributes 3,600 psalms to David, the book of Psalms attributes 73 to him, of which Psalm 145 is the last. We know that David loved music and musical instruments (1 Sam. 16:17–23; 2 Chron. 23:18). The Psalms mention a number of *instruments* used in worship. Psalm 150:3–5 lists a variety of instruments. What are they (see Ps. 33:2–3; 81:2–3; 92:2–3; 149:3)? The psalms also mention a number of *places* from which God can be praised. For example, look at Psalm 149:1, 5 and 150:1. What other places are mentioned?

Psalm 149:6–9 speaks of godly people judging the nations. Verse 9 begins, "to execute on them the judgment written!" Is this a prophecy referring to Revelation 19:11–21? If not, to what written judgment is the psalmist referring?

Read through the following three sections on *Gospel Glimpses, Whole-Bible Connections,* and *Theological Soundings.* Then take time to consider the *Personal Implications* these sections may have for you.

Gospel Glimpses

MERCIFUL ACCEPTANCE. The term "righteous" is commonly used in the Psalms to describe either the people of God in general (e.g., Ps. 125:3) or the faithful within the people (e.g., Ps. 140:13). In Psalm 143:1–2, however, the term is used to mean "qualified to stand in God's righteous presence" (see Rom. 4:9–11), and not even the faithful are that in themselves—"no one living is righteous before you" (Ps. 143:2). Therefore the psalmist's "pleas for mercy" (Ps. 143:1) are not only for relief from the immediate situation but also for God's merciful acceptance of him. Perfect righteousness is found only in Christ, who provides his own righteousness for those who are his (2 Cor. 5:21).

REDEMPTION. Throughout Israel's history (as vividly recounted and celebrated in Psalm 136), God has rescued and protected his people (see Ps. 44:26; 111:9; 130:7–8). For example, in the exodus, God redeemed Israel (i.e., bought back his people from Egyptian slavery). Through his death and resurrection, Jesus purchased redemption for all believers (Col. 1:13–14).

DELIVERANCE. Deliverance of Israel from its enemies prefigures Christ's deliverance from *his* enemies, both human and demonic (Matt. 26:46; Col. 2:15). It also prefigures our deliverance in Christ from sin, death, and Satan (Heb. 2:14–15).

Whole-Bible Connections

GOD'S KING. Psalm 144 talks about God's king (David) and how God trains his hands for war and subdues nations under him (vv. 1–2). Psalm 145 talks about God's kingdom (vv. 11, 12), which is "an everlasting kingdom" (v. 13). This language reflects Daniel's prophecy of God's kingship over his people administered through the Davidic Messiah (see Nebuchadnezzar's confession; Dan. 4:34). Jesus is that king!

LAST JUDGMENT. The devastation done to God's holy city Jerusalem, as recorded in Psalm 137, made God's people long for future blessing and for destruction to God's enemies, those who perpetrated that abominable act. God's ultimate answer to all evils will be found only in Christ's final judgment on the last day—when God's people will be saved and her enemies judged (Rev. 20:11–21:8).

EXECUTING GOD'S JUSTICE. Psalm 149 ends by calling to mind the expectation that the faithful will one day be God's agents of judgment through the world—"do you not know that the saints will judge the world?" (1 Cor. 6:2).

Theological Soundings

THE TONGUE. In Romans 3:13, Paul cites part of Psalm 140:3 in his argument that Jews and Greeks alike are "under sin" (Rom. 3:9). Psalm 141:3 offers a beautiful prayer concerning the tongue: "Set a guard, O LORD, over my mouth; keep watch over the door of my lips!" According to Jesus, our words are a reliable indicator of our spiritual health. Reprimanding the Pharisees, Jesus warns, "You brood of vipers! How can you speak good, when you are evil? For out of the abundance of the heart the mouth speaks. The good person out of his good treasure brings forth good, and the evil person out of his evil treasure brings forth evil. I tell you, on the day of judgment people will give account for every careless word they speak, for by your words you will be justified, and by your words you will be condemned" (Matt. 12:34–37).

TALION. According to the Old Testament, the punishment should match the crime (Gen. 9:6; Ex. 21:23–24). A notoriously difficult prayer for Christians to understand—"Blessed shall he be who takes your little ones and dashes them against the rock" (Ps. 137:9)—is based in part on this law. It is a prayer that the Babylonians, who had smashed Israelite infants, should be punished appropriately—in the same way.

Personal Implications

Take time to reflect on the implications of Psalms 135–150 for your own life today. Consider what you have learned that might lead you to praise God, repent of sin, and trust in his gracious promises. Make notes below on the personal implications for your walk with the Lord of the (1) *Gospel Glimpses*, (2) *Whole-Bible Connections*, (3) *Theological Soundings*, and (4) this passage as a whole.

1. Gospel Glimpses

2. Whole-Bible Connections

3. Theological Soundings

4. Psalms 135–150

As You Finish Studying Psalms . . .

We rejoice with you as you finish studying the book of Psalms! May this study become part of your Christian walk of faith, day by day and week by week throughout all your life. Now we would greatly encourage you to continue to study the Word of God on a week-by-week basis. To continue your study of the Bible, we would encourage you to consider other books in the *Knowing the Bible* series, and to visit www.knowingthebibleseries.org.

Lastly, take a moment again to look back through Psalms, which you have studied during these recent weeks. Review again the notes that you have written, and the things that you have highlighted or underlined. Reflect again on the key themes that the Lord has been teaching you about himself and about his Word. May these things become a treasure for you throughout your life—which we pray will be true for you, in the name of the Father, and the Son, and the Holy Spirit. Amen.

Definitions

[1] **Inclusio** – A common form of repetition used in Hebrew poetry, where the first and last verses of a poem have identical or nearly identical phrases or sentences.

[2] **Praise the Lord** – The Hebrew is one word—*Hallelu-yah* (English, Hallelujah).